James Kirke Paulding

Twayne's United States Authors Series

Lewis Leary, Editor

University of North Carolina, Chapel Hill

TUSAS 464

JAMES KIRKE PAULDING

(1778–1860)

Engraving by F.W. Halpin
after a drawing by Joseph Wood

James Kirke Paulding

By Larry J. Reynolds

Texas A&M University

Twayne Publishers • Boston

James Kirke Paulding
Larry J. Reynolds

Published by Twayne Publishers
A Division of G. K. Hall & Company
70 Lincoln Street
Boston, Massachusetts 02111

Book Production by Marne B. Sultz

Book Design by Barbara Anderson

Printed on permanent/durable acid-free paper and bound in the United States of America.

Library of Congress Cataloging in Publication Data

Reynolds, Larry J.
James Kirke Paulding.

(Twayne's United States authors series; TUSAS 464)
Bibliography: p. 150
Includes index.
1. Paulding, James Kirke, 1778–1860—Criticism and interpretation. I. Title. II. Series.
PS2528.R49 1984 818'.309 83-16629
ISBN 0-8057-7405-X

For my Father

Contents

About the Author
Preface
Chronology

Chapter One
Life 1

Chapter Two
Salmagundi Essays 20

Chapter Three
Anti-British Satires 39

Chapter Four
Poetry 55

Chapter Five
Literary Criticism 75

Chapter Six
Plays 93

Chapter Seven
Short Stories 103

Chapter Eight
Novels 113

Chapter Nine
Conclusion 135

Notes and References 139
Selected Bibliography 150
Index 155

About the Author

Larry J. Reynolds received the B.S. in Aerospace Engineering from the University of Cincinnati in 1966. While working as an Aeronautical Research Engineer with Battelle Columbus Laboratories, he earned the M.A. in English at Ohio State University, graduating in 1971. He subsequently studied at Duke University, specializing in nineteenth-century American literature, and he received the Ph.D. in English from Duke in 1974.

At present Dr. Reynolds is a Fulbright Lecturer on American Literature at the University of Oporto in Portugal and on leave of absence from Texas A&M University, where he is an Associate Professor of English. His publications include articles on Melville (in *American Literature, Studies in the Novel*, and *Melville Society Extracts*) on Melville and Hawthorne (in *American Transcendental Quarterly*), on Henry James (in *Studies in the Novel*), and on Welty (in the *Journal of Narrative Technique*).

Preface

Most modern readers, including many teachers of American literature, know nothing about the American writer James Kirke Paulding (1778–1860), a contemporary and friend of Washington Irving and James Fenimore Cooper; however, he deserves recognition for several reasons. First, as several Paulding scholars have pointed out, he was a pioneer in the establishment of an original American literature, leading the way in the use of American materials and American themes in his works, particularly those associated with the Indian and the New York Dutch. Second, he was an important figure in the major literary and political developments of his age, earning renown as an ardent participant in the Paper War with England, as an author of widely read satires, short stories, and novels, and as a fervent supporter of Jacksonian Democracy, eventually becoming Secretary of the Navy under President Van Buren. Finally, and most importantly, he deserves recognition for being a brilliant literary critic and, in several works, an outstanding artist. His critical essays contain some of the most original and thoughtful statements about literature to be found in nineteenth-century American criticism, while his novel *The Dutchman's Fireside* (1831) equals in narrative excellence anything written by Cooper or Simms. Not unimportantly, this novel and almost all of his best writings contain rich veins of humor, making them a joy to read.

During the 1820s and 1830s, Paulding was a best-selling author admired by critics on both sides of the Atlantic and spoken of in superlatives by Irving, Cooper, Poe, and Simms. His reputation waned during the rest of the nineteenth century, however, and only in the last thirty years has it undergone a modest revival. Since the early 1950s, a small but steady stream of articles, six dissertations, and Ralph M. Aderman's edition of Paulding's letters all have appeared. Despite this scholarly activity, however, no book-length study of Paulding's life or works has been published since 1926. Amos L. Herold's brief critical biography, which appeared in that year, is still a sound introduction to Paulding's career; nevertheless, there is an obvious need for a synthesis of recent Paulding scholarship and for a comprehensive new analysis of his best and most significant writings. The purpose of this book is to satisfy this need, with the intent of demonstrating not that Paulding is a neglected major writer, but rather that some of his achievements, in a variety of genres, are of major importance to American literary history. Chapter 1 of the book surveys Paulding's life, and subsequent chapters, forming an approximate chronological sequence, discuss his essays, satires, poetry, literary criticism, plays, short stories, and novels.

The opportunity to acknowledge formally the help of others is, I think, of much importance, so I am glad to take advantage of it here. I am grateful to the late Arlin Turner and to Richard Costa for encouraging me to undertake this project. The goodwill of William and Anne Owens and the hospitality of Benson and Mary Blake enabled me to spend the summer of 1978 conducting research in the Hudson River Valley. My department head, David Stewart, has been generally supportive and provided me with extra time to work on the project in the spring of 1979. Two mini-grants from Texas A&M University also gave me beneficial financial assistance.

I wish to thank the staffs of the Humanities Research Center at the University of Texas, the New Jersey Historical Society, Sleepy Hollow Restorations, the Charles Patterson Van Pelt Library at the University of Pennsylvania, the New York Public Library, and the Bancroft Library at the University of California at Berkeley. Halbert Hall and Mel Dodd of the Sterling C. Evans Library of Texas A&M University have been most helpful to me in locating and obtaining needed materials.

Anthony O'Keeffe, Norman Grabo, Merrill Whitburn, and Pamela Matthews read a portion of the manuscript, and I thank them for valuable responses. Ralph Aderman was kind enough to read the completed manuscript and to comment on it. I am deeply indebted to Tibbie Lynch and Katherine O'Keeffe for astute suggestions and kind encouragement. To Paul Parrish, whose criticism, counsel, and friendship I have depended upon from the beginning, I extend special thanks. My debt to my wife, Carol, is personal and comprehensive. My sons, Brian, Sean, and Robin, have my gratitude for their patience and love.

Larry J. Reynolds

Texas A&M University

Chronology

1778 James Kirke Paulding born August 22 at Pleasant Valley, New York.

ca. 1786 Goes to live with uncle; attends country school.

ca. 1796 Leaves Tarrytown and moves to New York City.

1807 Begins *Salmagundi* with Washington and William Irving.

1812 *The Diverting History of John Bull and Brother Jonathan.*

1813 *The Lay of the Scottish Fiddle.*

1814 Enlists in New York militia; commissioned a major.

1815 *The United States and England.* Appointed secretary of Board of Navy Commissioners; moves to Washington.

1816 Summer trip through Virginia.

1817 *Letters from the South.*

1818 Marries Gertrude Kemble on November 15. *The Backwoodsman.*

1819 Begins *Salmagundi, Second Series.*

1822 *A Sketch of Old England.*

1823 Resigns as secretary. *Koningsmarke.* Moves to New York City.

1824 Appointed Navy Agent for New York. Awarded honorary Master of Arts degree by Columbia.

1825 *John Bull in America.*

1826 *The Merry Tales of the Three Wise Men of Gotham.*

1827 Publishes "American Drama" and "York Town" articles.

1828 *The New Mirror for Travellers.*

1829 *Tales of the Good Woman.*

1830 Wins $300 prize for *The Lion of the West. Chronicles of the City of Gotham.*

1831 *The Dutchman's Fireside.*

1832 *Westward Ho! Tales of Glauber-Spa* (with others).

1835 *A Life of Washington.* Harpers begins publishing collected works.

1836 *Slavery in the United States. The Book of Saint Nicholas.*

1838 Appointed Secretary of the Navy. *A Gift from Fairy Land.*

1841 Retires from office. Wife dies.

1842 Trip through the South and West with Van Buren. Visits with Jackson at the Hermitage.

1845 Buys farm on the Hudson near Hyde Park.

1846 *The Old Continental.*

1847 *American Comedies* (with son William Irving).

1849 *The Puritan and His Daughter.*

1860 Dies April 6.

Chapter One

Life

Hudson River Valley Childhood and Youth

Paulding's best fiction, which anticipates the local-color writing and literary realism of later American writers, focuses on the people, places, and history of his native region.[1] "The Little Dutch Sentinel of the Manhadoes" (1827), "Cobus Yerks" (1828), and *The Dutchman's Fireside* (1831), his finest short stories and novel, all draw upon his intimate knowledge of the Hudson River Valley and its Dutch inhabitants and heritage. Unlike Irving, who was born with Engish ancestors and raised in the cosmopolitan society of New York City, Paulding was half Dutch and grew up in the provincial Sleepy Hollow country that Irving knew only as a visitor. Paulding's paternal grandfather, Joost or Joseph Jr., had moved from New York City to a farm two miles east of Tarrytown in 1753, and Paulding's father, William, after running away from home and spending a number of adventuresome years at sea, married and settled at Tarrytown about 1767. There, in the years before the Revolutionary War, he opened a store and became a prosperous trader and a prominent patriot.[2]

An ardent nationalism, composed of a love for his country and a hatred of England, dominates many of Paulding's writings and can certainly be traced in part to the circumstances surrounding his birth and early youth. He was born in the midst of the Revolution on August 22, 1778, at Pleasant Valley, New York, a place of family refuge some fifty-five miles north of Tarrytown. There his father, serving as Commissary General of the New York Militia, had removed his family to protect them from marauding bands of Yagers, Cow Boys, and Skinners, who roamed the "Neutral Ground" between the British forces in New York City and the American Army in the Hudson Highlands.

At the conclusion of the war, the Pauldings returned to Tarrytown, and as the young James listened to accounts of recent events told by relatives and neighbors, he learned much about British perfidy and American heroism. Nine members of his family, including his father and three uncles, had served in the American Army, and his first cousin, John Paulding, and his brother-in-law, Isaac Requa, had suffered confinement in the infamous British prisons of New York. Two other relatives, both noncombatants, also suffered at the hands of the enemy. Paulding's Aunt Sarah, John Paulding's mother, had her house plundered by a party of British cow thieves while her husband and son were away and, according to a local historian, was "compelled to submit to indignities," which remain unspecified.[3] In addition, Paulding's maternal grandfather, Nathaniel Ogden, was savagely cut across the head by a party of British soldiers because he would not cry "God save the King," and his brain was permanently damaged by the blow. Years later, Paulding related that "one of the earliest, as well as most painful recollections, of my childhood, is the figure of this aged man.... I remember him walking along the beach at Tarrytown, picking up sticks, and talking to himself about the reign of Queen Anne . . . and how the Tories were no better than highway robbers."[4] In the novel *Westward Ho!* (1832), Paulding included a brief scene based on this recollection, with the wounded old man placing a potent curse upon his attacker.

During Paulding's childhood, these sources of sad and bitter memories were somewhat balanced by stories of his cousin John's heroism, which came to occupy a central spot in Paulding's adult imagination. Tall, young, and daring, John on September 23, 1780, along with two friends, David Williams and Isaac Van Wart, captured the British spy Major André, found the plans to West Point in his boot, resisted his attempt to bribe them, and thus foiled General Benedict Arnold's treasonous plans. In a number of his writings, Paulding alluded to the capture of André with a mixture of pride and indignation; he found it particularly offensive that the aristocratic British spy became a romantic figure in American thought and art, while the three American farmer-soldiers, poor but honest, became forgotten heroes. A spur to his indignation was the denunciation of John and the two others in 1817 by Colonel Benjamin Tallmadge, a former Revolutionary officer (who had custody of André after his capture) and a current member of the House of

Representatives. To explain his opposition to the fifty-eight-year-old John Paulding's request for an increase in his pension, Tallmadge characterized the three captors as Cow Boys out on a plundering expedition, adding that Major André had assured him he would have been released if he could have satisfied their thirst for money.[5] In his poem *The Backwoodsman* (1818) and his satire *The New Mirror for Travellers, and Guide to the Springs* (1828), Paulding praised the three and criticized Tallmadge. In 1846 he then paid high tribute to his cousin in the novel *The Old Continental* by modeling his hero on him and using the capture of André as the climax of the narrative.

The war that brought bitterness and pride to Paulding and his family eventually brought poverty as well. During the Revolution, Paulding's father, responsible for supplying the American Army in Peekskill, pledged his own property with the farmers of Westchester and Dutchess counties when they would no longer accept the worthless Continental money being issued by the new government. After the war, when he applied to the state legislature and then Congress for reimbursement, it was denied him. He had not had official authorization for his actions, he was told. Consequently, he lost all he owned and was confined as a debtor in a log prison at White Plains, while his wife and nine children were forced to fend for themselves.

Needless to say, William Paulding's ruin and imprisonment greatly affected his young son James. The passionate condemnation of paper money to be found everywhere in Paulding's works plus his spirited support of Andrew Jackson's war against the banks were influenced by his father's fate. Also, one suspects that the proud independence and reserve that characterized Paulding's adult personality had their origins in the trauma caused by his father's confinement. At the young age of seven or eight, he was sent every Saturday to the prison, some six miles away, on an old borrowed horse with a supply of clean clothes and a few necessary items the family could afford. "It was a melancholy journey," Paulding wrote late in life, "and I cannot think on it, even at this distant period, without painful emotions."[6]

Although the prison burned down after several months and William Paulding was allowed to walk home a free man, his life had been irreparably damaged, as had his family's. As Paulding explains in the autobiographical story "Dyspepsy" (1829), his father lapsed into an inactive state, reading, watching the stars, and waiting for Continental money to be worth something, while the large family was cared for by Paulding's mother, who heroically supported them by her sewing. The considerable poverty Paulding endured during these years is probably the main reason why as an adult he adopted a commercial attitude toward his writing; to put it bluntly, he wrote for money, with the result that much of his voluminous work is lusterless due to a lack of polish. He also died a wealthy man, however, and his own family was always well provided for. During his lifetime, he earned more than $50,000 from his writings, and at his death his estate was probably worth between $50,000 and $80,000.[7]

The poverty of Paulding's family resulted also in his receiving little formal education, a circumstance that may explain the narrow, rugged, and independent nature of his thought. For a portion of three or four years, he attended a country school, held in a log hut about two miles from his home. One day the schoolmaster, having been appointed a county official, abruptly dismissed his students and left. "Thus ended my education," Paulding wrote, "which first and last cost about fifteen dollars, certainly quite as much as it was worth." Actually his education continued, but it was self-designed and informal. Thanks to the example of his father, Paulding loved to read, and although only a few books survived the family's financial disaster, these became treasures in his eyes and led him to acquire several beneficial habits. "What I read I read thoroughly," he later recalled, "and what I learned I learned well."[8]

While Paulding went to school, he stayed with his aunt and uncle on their farm near the Sawmill River several miles east of Tarrytown, and in their house he discovered one book that significantly shaped his thought and art, Oliver Goldsmith's *The Citizen of the World* (1762). "I read it, I believe twenty times at least," he wrote, "and if I have any taste or style, I owe them to that charming work of the most delightful of all English writers."[9] Goldsmith's book, which satirizes native customs by having a foreign traveler describe them, gave Paulding not only taste and style, but also a model for many of his satiric works. He also seems to have followed Goldsmith's example in the shaping of his own career, making versatility—that is, the writing of essays, novels, satires, poetry, plays—its most noticeable feature.

Although we do not know what other writers Paulding read and admired during his youth, we can infer from the techniques employed and allusions found in his works that he must have become familiar, at some time before he began his literary career, with Addison, Fielding, Swift, Dryden, and Pope. They, along with Goldsmith, taught him to write with clarity and simplicity, to appreciate the power of satire and irony, and to distrust the emerging romantic emphasis on emotion and sensation.

During his school days, Paulding developed into a lonely, introverted, and melancholy boy. He walked alone the two miles to and from his school each day, and at the farm he had as his only companion a mute girl, the daughter of an old soldier living on a corner of his uncle's property. Forty years later, Paulding drew upon his memories of this girl in his portrait of Phoebe Angevine in "The Dumb Girl" (1830), his most pathetic and moving tale. During this dreary stage of his life, he also was ill and overcome by a fear of death. Thus physically and emotionally weakened, he was profoundly disturbed, almost to the point of madness, while attending a religious revival. This experience no doubt contributed to his later denunciations of religious fanaticism and served as the source for the climactic scenes in *Westward Ho!* (1832) and "The Mother's Tragedy" (1846) where the protagonists lose their sanity under the influence of ranting revival preachers.

Curiously, during Paulding's teenage years, he did not seek employment nor work at a paying job. In "Dyspepsy" he attributes this to the influence of his mother, who "could not forget old times, nor bear the idea that her only son should learn a trade, or slave in any useful occupation."[10] Although not an only son, Paulding did become, as he elsewhere acknowledged, "the most conspicuous idler in the village,"[11] and he spent his days reading, thinking, daydreaming, and roaming at random through the beautiful woods, glens, and fields near his Tarrytown home.

During these years he acquired a deep love of nature, and his halfhearted attempts at hunting, fishing, and trapping served as excuses for being out-of-doors. As a boy he lived very much in a world of his own creation, and his love of nature seems to have grown out of his dreamy and imaginative view of the material world. Although his writings are filled with passages describing the rivers, hills, skies, and forests of the American landscape, these descriptions are often vague and sentimental. Like the Hudson River School of painters, whom his works inspired, Paulding held romantic preconceptions about nature that prevented him from viewing it with the objectivity and precision of the naturalist. Death, decay, and the ruthlessness of nature's way usually play no part in the pleasant settings he describes, except when such facts are included for some unnatural, melodramatic effect.

What Paulding called his "*unnatural*, admiration of Nature" (*Letters*, 22) accounts not only for the prominence of natural description in his works, but also for the conservative agrarianism at the center of his social and political thought. He would always believe in the moral superiority of the rural life, even while living some forty-eight years in the cities of New York and Washington, and this belief in turn led him to praise the small farmer, the southern planter, the frontier settler and to criticize speculators, abolitionists, reformers, and advocates of progress in general. Significantly, when he retired, he turned to the life he had idealized in his works by becoming a farmer on a country estate overlooking the Hudson.

Apprenticeship with the Irvings in New York City

In 1796 or 1797, when he was about eighteen, Paulding left Tarrytown and went to New York City, where he spent the next eighteen years of his life, there developing from a shy, country boy into a sociable, satiric Knickerbocker. In New York he first lived with his sister Julia and her husband, William Irving, the oldest brother of Washington and a man toward whom Paulding felt much respect and affection. Paulding's own older brother William, a lawyer who would become Mayor of New York in 1823, secured him a job as a clerk in the United States Loan Office and, along with the Irvings, introduced the young man into New York society.

Although New York was then a town of only some sixty thousand, reaching just two miles north of the Battery with here and there country roads and open fields, its mixed population was growing rapidly and its shops, theaters, hotels, and taverns were crowded and bustling. By all accounts, the social atmosphere of the day was particularly lively, with plays, parties, dances, and concerts forming an important part of New York City life. In addition, numerous clubs and societies, which met at gathering places such as the Fraunces

Tavern, Charles Wiley's bookstore, and Bixby's Hotel provided clever young men like Paulding the opportunity to drink and socialize together, to discuss books, plays, and politics, and to refine their own literary talents.

In this atmosphere Paulding flourished. He established lifelong friendships and acquired a skill and penchant for writing that soon led to literary success. He joined the Debating Society and probably participated in the older and more illustrious Calliopean Society, which met for a time at the home of its leading member, William Irving. The programs of both societies were devoted to composition, recitation, oration, and debate, with members officially charged with criticizing each other's efforts.[12] For Paulding these activities represented a painful education. "I was excessively thin-skinned," he later recalled, "and nothing was so painful to me as ridicule. They broke me in by quizzing me most unmercifully. . . . It was a rough discipline to a lad of my temperament, but proved of great service in after-life; and, though I look back on it with something like horror, I have always considered the lessons worth the purchase. It was the best school in which I ever studied."[13]

During the early 1800s, Paulding and his closest friends formed a loose social fraternity called the "Lads of Kilkenny"; the members, all of whom had nicknames, included Washington, Peter, and Ebenezer Irving, Henry Brevoort, Jr., David Porter, Henry Ogden, Richard McCall, and Gouverneur Kemble. The Lads shared a love for festivity and refreshment, and they would gather at Dyde's Tavern in Park Row or, when their funds were low, at a porterhouse at the corner of John and Nassau Streets, where they would spend their evenings eating, drinking, and singing, eventually becoming drunk and riotous. On the weekends, they traveled by stage to Gouverneur Kemble's family mansion on the banks of the Passaic, between Newark and Belleville, and here they drank, played leapfrog on the lawn, flirted with the Belleville girls, and indulged in highjinks that they recalled with much nostalgic pleasure in later years.[14]

Although Paulding was naturally shy and reserved, he learned to enjoy New York society. In fact, in March 1808, Irving informed a mutual friend in Philadelphia that "[Jim] has become quite a tea-party hero," ready to "assist at all the conventions of Petticoats."[15] After Paulding first arrived in New York, Irving had become his best friend and, although four and a half years younger, had taught him to appreciate fashionable young ladies, good fellowship, the theater, and professional writing. The two had met several times as boys in Tarrytown, where they explored the Sleepy Hollow region together, fishing along the brooks, although Irving, according to Paulding, lacked patience and thus "was beyond question the worst fisherman we ever knew."[16] During their years together in New York City before Irving went to Europe in 1815 for a seventeen-year stay, they read and criticized each other's manuscripts and planned several joint literary ventures.

Both first saw their writings in print in Peter Irving's *Morning Chronicle* (1802–1805), a New York newspaper that published Irving's letters written under the pseudonym "Jonathan Oldstyle, Gent." and contributions by Paulding written under the pseudonym "Walter Withers."[17] From January 24, 1807, to January 25, 1808, they joined with William Irving in publishing *Salmagundi*, a series of twenty pamphlets that satirized the contemporary New York scene, particularly fashionable dandies, scantily clad young ladies, French dancing masters, and, occasionally, President Jefferson as well. *Salmagundi* captured the convivial spirit of the times and was an immediate popular success. Although Washington Irving later disdained it as a "juvenile production,"[18] Paulding always regarded it fondly and in 1819–1820 wrote *Salmagundi, Second Series* by himself.

Paulding obviously learned and gained much from his early association with Irving and valued him as a dear friend throughout his life; however, in many ways the association undermined his own literary reputation. Because the two authors collaborated on a successful venture and dealt in their own works with similar subjects such as the New York Dutch, Hudson River Valley scenery, the Indians, and the life of George Washington, many critics, in their lifetimes and since, have compared the two and relegated Paulding to an inferior position. Such comparisons reveal, as Irving privately lamented, a lack of understanding of his and Paulding's "distinct and comparative merit."[19] While the genial atmosphere and graceful style of Irving's better works are unmatched by Paulding's more rugged and unpolished achievements, one nevertheless finds in Paulding's best writings a superlative originality, vitality, and acuity that have gone unnoticed by those viewing him as a mere shadow of his more famous and popular friend.

Participation in the Paper War with England

We know little about Paulding's life between 1808 and 1812, but we do know that in 1809 he helped Irving prepare for publication *A History of New York, by Diedrich Knickerbocker* and that in 1812 the two men, who were living in Mrs. Bradish's boarding house at the time, planned another joint literary venture that never was completed. Also during this period, Paulding apparently became more and more interested in the political life of the nation and the approaching conflict with England, "Mr. Madison's War" as it was called by Federalist New Englanders. In 1812 he published his first book, *The Diverting History of John Bull and Brother Jonathan*, a satirical political allegory that personifies the national characters of England and the United States and humorously explains the course of international affairs in terms of human emotions such as jealousy, pride, and familial love-hate. The allegory, for the most part anti-British, portrays England as an overbearing old fool and represents Paulding's first major contribution to the Anglo-American controversy known as the Paper War, a battle of words fought by writers on both sides of the Atlantic for some fifty years following the Revolution.

During the next thirty-four years, Paulding remained on the front lines in the "war." In 1813, he published a poem entitled *The Lay of the Scottish Fiddle*, which parodied Scott's *Lay of the Last Minstrel* and described with patriotic indignation the burning of Havre de Grace, Maryland, by the British. In 1814 he became a major in the New York militia,[20] and in the same year his poem *The Lay* was published in London and viciously attacked by the prestigious *Quarterly Review.* This journal, at the same time, in a review of C. J. Ingersoll's *Inchiquin's Letters* (1810), published a malicious commentary on American manners, customs, politics, and people, which inspired Paulding's next anti-British work, *The United States and England* (1815). This book, actually a long pamphlet, refutes the *Quarterly*'s criticism point by point, and in it one can see the maturation of Paulding's nationalist sympathies.

In a letter to Brevoort, Irving privately made fun of Paulding's anglophobia, and in *The Sketch Book* he publicly opposed Paulding's nationalism by declaring: "We are a young people, necessarily an imitative one, and must take our examples and models, in a great degree, from the existing nations of Europe. There is no country more worthy of our study than England."[21] It was Paulding's indipendent spirit, rather than Irving's dependent one, however, that eventually led to the American literary renaissance, or more accurately naissance, that occurred around mid-century. As part of his defense of American life and culture, Paulding argued that the American writer should reject English models and contribute to America's literary independence "by freeing himself from a habit of servile imitation; by daring to think and feel, and express his feelings; by dwelling on scenes and events connected with our pride and our affections."[22] While writers such as Hawthorne, Melville, Whitman, and Twain would be most successful in such efforts, Paulding himself was one of the first to put his theories into practice.

As he was battling with British detractors of America, particularly British reviewers and travel writers, Paulding began to write about events connected with American pride by contributing accounts of American naval victories and biographies of American naval heroes to the *Analectic Magazine*, which Irving edited in 1813 and 1814. Although these essays represent hack work of sorts, they, along with *The United States and England*, attracted the attention of President Madison and led to Paulding's appointment as secretary of the Board of Navy Commissioners, the first of a series of political appointments he received without solicitation. In 1815 he went to Washington, where he would live for the next eight years; at about the same time he published a satire on banks and paper currency entitled *The History of the Little Frenchman and His Bank Notes*, all copies of which have evidently disappeared.[23]

For the most part Paulding found the small-town atmosphere of Washington oppressive. The petty gossip of its women irritated him; the political sycophancy of its men depressed him; and the uncivilized remoteness of its location bored him. Although he became friends with a number of important politicians, including President Madison, Speaker of the House Henry Clay, and Congressman John Randolph, Paulding nevertheless thought of himself as an outsider of sorts, a Knickerbocker bemused by the Washington political scene and nostalgic for the conviviality and fellowship he enjoyed in New York. The nostalgic note sounded in his letters during these years became a persistent strain in his future works, and from 1815 on,

Paulding became a man who in many ways idealized the past at the same time he was very much involved in events of the present.

His job as secretary again allowed him time for writing and travel, and in 1816 he spent several months vacationing in Virginia to restore his health. This trip led to his next book, *Letters from the South* (1817), made up of a series of epistolary essays on miscellaneous topics ranging from mountain scenery to the evils of slavery, paper money, and city life. The trip also stimulated his interest in regions of America outside of his native New York and inspired his writing of *The Backwoodsman* (1818), a long poem in heroic couplets that attempts to glorify the American pioneer and to describe the scenery and inhabitants of the American West (which at the time was Ohio). In this work Paulding also broke new literary ground by treating the plight of the Indian with an understanding undiluted by sentimentality.

In the spring of 1818, at the age of thirty-nine, Paulding wrote Irving that he had decided on writing as a vocation for the remainder of his life. In the fall of that same year, after a two-year engagement, he married Gertrude Kemble, the sister of his friend Gouverneur Kemble and daughter of Peter Kemble, a retired New York merchant. After setting up a home with his new bride in a small three-story brick house on Pennsylvania Avenue, a gift from Gertrude's father, Paulding revived *Salmagundi*, to Irving's dismay, and from May 30, 1819, to September 2, 1820, he published fifteen numbers, composed for the most part of social satire, character sketches, and sentimental tales of woe. The series, though well written, was scorned by reviewers, who compared it unfavorably to the first *Salmagundi* and to Irving's *The Sketch Book*, which also appeared in installments during 1819 and 1820. The most important of Paulding's numbers was the last, for it contained the essay "The Wreck of Genius" (later condensed and retitled "National Literature"), in which he sets forth his program for a native American literature and introduces his theory of "Rational Fictions," which anticipated by some sixty years the defense of literary realism by Howells, Twain, and James.

In 1822 Paulding published his next anti-British book, *A Sketch of Old England by A New-England Man*, which attempts to turn the tables on English travelers whose critical accounts of America were based on uninformed and biased observations. The satire of the book is weak, however, and its tone vicious; late in life Paulding acknowledged and regretted the "gall and bitterness" (*Letters*, 548) with which it is filled.

Reign as Popular Author

In 1823 Paulding's wife received a sizeable inheritance from her father's estate, and Paulding resigned his Washington job and moved his family back to New York City to live in the Kemble mansion in Whitehall Street. At this time, he apparently felt ready to act upon his decision to make writing his vocation, and during the next fifteen years he did just that, with remarkable success. Between 1823 and 1838, he authored three novels, five volumes of short stories, two satires, a play, a biography, and a treatise on slavery.

During approximately six weeks he spent in Washington by himself while his family was in New York City, he wrote his first novel, *Koningsmarke* (1823), a historical romance treating the early Swedish settlers in Delaware and the Indians of central Pennsylvania. The novel's nine parts are preceded by introductory chapters similar to those in Fielding's *Tom Jones*, and in them Paulding satirizes romantic conventions in general and Sir Walter Scott in particular. Although the novel as a whole seems uncertain in purpose and inconsistent in tone, it contains sharp humor and powerful dramatic scenes involving the Indians.

Soon after his return to New York, Paulding was appointed Navy Agent for New York by President Monroe, a position that again demanded little of his time thanks to his chief clerk, George L. Storer, a diligent soul who handled the day-to-day workings of the Agency. Although Paulding did not solicit the appointment, one suspects his brother William's recent election to Mayor of New York City spoke silently in his behalf. In August 1824, Paulding received additional recognition when Columbia College awarded him an honorary Master of Arts degree for his literary accomplishments.

While achieving professional success, Paulding experienced much personal tragedy and grief. Within an eight-year period he lost his father, William Paulding, Sr. (1735–1825), his son William Irving (1821–1825), two daughters, both named Mary Kemble (1824–1827 and 1827–1828), and his mother, Catharine Ogden (1742–1830). Paulding prided himself on his stoicism, and he refused to let these events devastate him. Instead, he kept on writing, which served as therapy of sorts. His last anti-British book, *John Bull in America* (1825), was written as his young son was dying; it was, he told Irving, "the product of a season of gloomy anticipation—of intervals of watching and nursing our poor boy" (*Letters*, 82). Surprisingly, the book, which satirizes once again the ignorance, stupidity, and pomposity of the British traveler in America, is one of Paulding's most humorous works, filled with delightful caricature and rousing tall tales.

For the most part, Paulding's literary energies in the late 1820s were expended in writing short works. Amos L. Herold has called the years 1824–1832 "the Paulding decade of the short story,"[24] for during this period he published some forty stories and sketches in the leading annual and the leading weekly of the day, the *Atlantic Souvenir* and the *New-York Mirror*; however, only a few are of high quality. He brought out most of his published stories plus a few new ones in collections entitled *Tales of the Good Woman* (1829) and *Chronicles of the City of Gotham* (1830). He also wrote two contributions for the collection *Tales of Glauber-Spa* (1832), which contained stories by Catharine M. Sedgwick and William Cullen Bryant, among others.

Two of the books he published during this period contain now rather dated satire of the contemporary social scene. *The Merry Tales of the Three Wise Men of Gotham* (1826) is directed at Robert Owen's idea of human perfectibility, the courts and the law, and phrenology; *The New Mirror for Travellers, and Guide to the Springs* (1828) burlesques current guide books and pokes fun at the fashionable set who vacationed at Ballston and Saratoga during the late 1820s. Paulding's liveliest and most enduringly humorous effort during this time was his play *The Lion of the West* (1830), featuring the hilarious Nimrod Wildfire, modeled on David Crockett and first acted on the stage by the outstanding comic actor of the day, James H. Hackett. The play, which won Hackett's prize for the most original American comedy, was very well received and became a successful part of Hackett's repertory for more than twenty years.

The year 1831 marked the highpoint of Paulding's literary career, for it saw the publication of his finest work, the novel *The Dutchman's Fireside*, which achieved exceptional popularity immediately following its publication, going through six editions within a year and being translated into five European languages within seven years. While portraying old Dutch life on the Hudson, it details the maturation of a shy, awkward boy, Sybrandt Westbrook, who becomes a courageous, self-possessed man through his confrontations with the Indians, the wilderness, and British soldiers. The novel's realism, local color, and engaging central theme, dealing with the complex struggle between Doric simplicity and Corinthian artifice, make the work an outstanding achievement that has just begun to receive the critical attention it deserves.

Paulding's next novel, *Westward Ho!* (1832), attempts again to portray American settings and American themes. The first half of the novel focuses on the adventures of the Dangerfield family, who move from their home in Virginia to the Kentucky frontier, while the second half treats the psychological problems of Dudley Rainsford, the lover of Colonel Dangerfield's daughter, Virginia. Although the novel lacks the realistic sense of place that distinguishes *The Dutchman's Fireside*, several of Paulding's characters are skillfully drawn, particularly his frontiersman Ambrose Bushfield; also, the attempt to deal with abnormal psychology is for the most part successful and anticipates the psychological realism of Hawthorne.

During the mid-1830s, Paulding turned to nonfiction in several books. His *Life of Washington* (1835) was written for children under a contract by which Harper & Brothers agreed to distribute 5,000 copies in the public schools. Inspired by a deep respect for the character of Washington, it is more reliable and better written than previous biographies of the day. The book went through ten editions before 1858 and was considered the standard biography of Washington before being superseded by Irving's monumental study published in 1855 through 1859. Poe was impressed by the work, declaring that "it would be difficult, even with great care and labor, to improve upon the general manner of the volumes now before us . . . they contain many long individual passages of a force and beauty not to be surpassed by the finest passages of the finest writers in any time or country."[25] Most readers of the biography today will find it too general and uncritical.

Paulding's other major work of nonfiction, *Slavery in the United States* (1836), was a political treatise which defended the southern view of an issue that had become highly controversial. Although he sympathized with the plight of the Negro, Paulding argued, like many other thoughtful men of his day, that the dissolution of the Union would result in far greater evil than slavery itself. Beneath this argument can be perceived the racist attitude Paulding slowly adopted toward blacks and toward the Indians as well. His tendency to think of both as inherently inferior to whites eventually formed one of the most unattractive aspects of his character, and occasionally undermined, through his use of racial stereotypes, the integrity of his fiction as well.

After publishing his nonfiction books, Paulding brought out two more collections of short stories. Those in *The Book of Saint Nicholas* (1836 or 1837)[26] are based on old Dutch folklore and show Paulding handling local color, plot, and characterization with admirable artistry. His *A Gift from Fairy Land* (1838), however, is a slick collection of four slight fairy tales intended to capitalize on the lucrative gift-book market of the day.

By the late 1830s, Paulding had become more and more involved in party politics, writing anonymous pieces on behalf of the Democratic administration in the *Evening Post.* These efforts stemmed in part from his interest in his friend Martin Van Buren's presidential prospects, but he also believed in the rightness of the stands being taken by the Jackson administration on banks, slavery, internal improvements, and the removal of the Indians from Georgia and Alabama. As he approached the age of sixty, Paulding became more and more sure of himself, some would say more opinionated, and quicker to express his opinions through the newspapers. In a letter to Irving in 1836, he justified his contributions on behalf of "the good cause," by observing that "If men of good principles keep aloof from all participation in Newspapers, they will naturally fall into the hands of interested factions, and unprincipled demagogues, and become their instruments of mischief" (*Letters*, 188).

By the fall of 1837, Paulding's party fervor had become so heated that Van Buren cautioned him to be cooler, and he agreed to do so. In the spring of 1838, Van Buren then rewarded Paulding's services to the party by offering him a cabinet position as Secretary of the Navy after Mahlon Dickerson, the incumbent, resigned and Jacob Sutherland and Washington Irving declined the post.

Secretary of the Navy

Although Paulding's party loyalty and his friendship with Van Buren were important factors in his cabinet appointment, which he accepted after some hesitation, he was well qualified for the office; he had to his credit a firm grasp of national problems, twenty years involvement in naval matters, and proven abilities as an administrator. From the outset, he handled his new job with confidence and reforming zeal, acting quickly to restore discipline to the Navy and to curtail the practice of granting special treatment to high naval officers and to those with connections in government circles. Not surprisingly, he soon became quite unpopular, but he seems to have taken a grim satisfaction in his unpopularity. Throughout his life, he had a tendency to be self-righteous (as perhaps all satirists do), and it shone through in his handling of his office and his disregard for his critics.

During his three years in office, Paulding dealt with a number of administrative tasks that left him little time for writing. He oversaw the preparations and launching of the South Sea Exploring Expedition under the command of Charles Wilkes, initiated the building of a dry dock at New York, ardently recommended the establishment of a naval academy, and worked to obtain better iron for anchors and quality American-made hemp. Having little regard for the idea of "progress" and nostalgic affection for the old sailing ships, he also staunchly resisted the movement to develop a steamship navy but eventually yielded to the demands of the public and Congress by supervising the building of two steam frigates, *The Missouri* and *The Mississippi.*

While in office, Paulding was harshly attacked in print, and the abuse he received probably influenced the decline in his literary reputation after he retired from politics. In response to the publication of his collected works by Harper & Brothers in 1835–1839, N. P. Willis asserted that Paulding the author was "quite dead and forgotten." Calling him the "jackal" of Irving, Willis asked "how in the name of wonder did these twelve volumes of flat, pointless, and essentially vulgar stuff ever find printer, publisher, puffer, and reader!"[27] Paulding was defended by Colonel James Watson Webb in the *New York Courier & Enquirer*, and, more significantly, William Gilmore Simms, partly in response to Willis's attack, dedicated his novel *The Damsel of Darien* (1839) "TO THE HON. JAMES

K. PAULDING, As one of the earliest pioneers in the field of American letters, as one of the ablest and most patriotic. . . ." Nevertheless, the attacks by Willis and others did considerable damage to Paulding's reputation, and after leaving Washington, he was never thought of as highly as a writer as before he went there.

Irving had had the prescience to see that this could happen to an individual, for when declining the position that Paulding accepted, he cited his inability to endure "the bitter personal hostility, and the slanders and misrepresentations of the press, which beset high station in this country."[28] Soon after taking office, Paulding wrote Irving, "You did right in the course you took and I sometimes think I too Should have done right in following your example" (*Letters*, 221). When it became apparent in 1840 that the Whigs with their Log Cabin and Hard Cider campaign would defeat Van Buren's bid for a second term, Paulding looked forward to retirement with a sense of relief. "Public stations," he wrote Gouverneur Kemble, "are becoming little better than pillories, in which a man is set up to be pelted with old shoes and rotten eggs" (*Letters*, 286).

Retirement

Before settling in a permanent home after leaving Washington, Paulding spent four years getting his bearings. The death of his wife in the spring of 1841 left him with four sons, ages seven to twenty-one, to care for. During the rest of that year, he remained in seclusion in New York City writing anonymous articles in support of Van Buren for the *Washington Globe* and the *New York Evening Post.*

In February of 1842, he accompanied Van Buren on a 7,000-mile trip through the South and the West. The trip, which Paulding considered a vacation, was perceived by everyone as Van Buren's attempt to gain southern support for the next election. The two men visited with Joel Poinsett in North Carolina, then after traveling by stage to New Orleans and by steamboat to Nashville, they visited with Andrew Jackson at the Hermitage. On their return home by way of the Mississippi and the Great Lakes, they also visited with Henry Clay in Ashland, Kentucky, where the two presidential candidates apparently agreed to keep the question of the annexation of Texas out of the campaign, which led to their defeats.

The stay with Jackson was the high point of the trip for Paulding, who later wrote that Jackson was "the only man I ever saw that excited my admiration to the pitch of wonder."[29] A secondary reward was Paulding's opportunity to see new regions of the country, which he later described in three magazine articles: "The Mississippi," "Sketch of the Great Western Lakes," and "The Illinois and the Prairies."

After Van Buren's hopes for reelection were dashed by the nomination of Polk at the 1844 Democratic Party Convention, Paulding, at the age of sixty-seven, began looking for a farm in the Hudson Highlands where he might spend his remaining years. In the summer of 1845, he bought an estate just a few miles north of Hyde Park overlooking the Hudson. There he turned his attention to farming and viewed with detachment and conservative disdain the affairs of state that for many years had engaged his intense interest.

In his retirement Paulding once again began writing stories and essays for the magazines and found time to write two novels, *The Old Continental* (1846) and *The Puritan and His Daughter* (1849). With his son William, he also brought out a volume of plays entitled *American Comedies* (1847), but Paulding's one contribution to the volume, *The Bucktails*, is a comedy of manners he had written thirty-five years previously.

The Old Continental is an interesting but badly flawed novel. It focuses on the adventures of Paulding's cousin John during the Revolution and compares favorably with Cooper's *The Spy* (1821) in its portrayal of the "Neutral Ground." Paulding's descriptions of the rural countryside, the American troops wintering in the Highlands, and the conditions on the British prison ships in New York City are admirably vivid and realistic. Unfortunately his characters lack the credibility of his settings, and his plot is marred by an anticlimactic ending. Paulding's last book, *The Puritan and His Daughter*, shows an even greater falling off of his imaginative and compositional abilities. It was Paulding's favorite work, yet it is probably his weakest; its structure is rambling, its characters wooden, and its main theme (concerning the liberating spirit of the West versus the intolerance of Old and New England) undeveloped.

When Paulding died on April 6, 1860, at the age of eighty-two, he was a forgotten man in many ways. His books were out of print, and his particular brand of conservatism held no attraction for the new generation of romantic writers and radical thinkers. In the letters written during his last years, he expressed disdain for the Transcendentalists, and they, had they known, would not have cared in the least. Even the writers who benefited from Paulding's example did not seem to know it. As early as 1850, Herman Melville could call on America to recognize her own writers and throw off the yoke of England with no apparent sense of echoing Paulding's outspokenness of some thirty years earlier. Similarly, by 1867 William Dean Howells could dismiss Paulding as "an old-fashioned mannerist,"[30] and yet in the 1880s proceed to define and call for a literary realism in terms remarkably similar to Paulding's own, expressed some fifty years previously.

Some responsibility for the disdain and neglect Paulding suffered after his death belongs to his son William I. Paulding, whose modest and curiously apologetic biography of 1867 did less than nothing to revive his father's reputation. "In justice to the talents of the man," William wrote in his Preface, "it should be observed that he was in no exact sense an author. . . . His adventures in literature proper were rather the episodes of his intellectual activity than the real labors of his mind."[31] In trying not to overestimate his father's achievement, William erred in the opposite direction.

Paulding himself knew that much he had written deserved to be forgotten, but he also suspected that some of his writings had "the principle of vitality in them" and would "revive at some time or other." These sentiments were expressed in an 1855 letter he wrote to his friend George P. Morris; he also told Morris, "Though left in the rear in the first heats, we have *good bottom* and I predict, will come in at the last round ahead of some of the 'Eclipses' " (*Letters*, 552). Since the early 1950s, Paulding's significant contributions to the development of an original American literature have begun to be recognized and appreciated; in the chapters that follow the particular nature of these contributions will be examined.

Chapter Two

Salmagundi Essays

Salmagundi, First Series

Perhaps the greatest irony of Paulding's career is that his first major literary venture, as the product of collaboration with Washington Irving, endowed him with the small literary fame that he now has, yet also led to the rather severe underestimation of his literary accomplishments. Although Paulding's contribution to American literature was considerable, since the early 1820s, critics have insisted upon aligning his work with Irving's and seeing it in eclipse as a result.

Inception. *Salmagundi; or, the Whim-Whams and Opinions of Launcelot Langstaff, Esq. and Others* was a periodical of twenty numbers that appeared at irregular intervals between January 24, 1807, and January 25, 1808. According to Paulding's recollection at the age of sixty-seven, it grew out of a conversation between himself and Irving when they were youths:

> We were both under twenty, [he wrote,] when one day in a frolicksome mood, we broached the Idea of a little Periodical merely for our own Amusement, and that of the Town, for neither of us anticipated any further circulation. We each without concert, prepared an introductory Paper, and I think mine was taken as the basis, with Mr. Irving's for the Superstructure. The first number, though it seemed to su[r]prise the Town, astonished us still more. In short it circulated throughout the United States, and most unquestionably did much to awaken the genius of the Country, by exciting emulation. It was the work in fact of two Boys, and when I chance to look into it now, I am surprised at its faults more than its beauties. (*Letters*, 426)

A combination of modesty and pride makes Paulding's account here slightly misleading, for elsewhere he revealed a paternal fondness for the work (although Irving disdained it). Also, it was no teenage lark.

At the beginning of 1807 when *Salmagundi* was conceived, Paulding was a twenty-eight-year-old clerk in the United States Loan Office who had already written his satirical pieces for the *Morning Chronicle* and the *Town.* Irving was a twenty-four-year-old lawyer who had likewise written his Jonathan Oldstyle letters for the *Morning Chronicle* and possibly as many as forty-five satirical pieces that appeared in the *Corrector* in March and April of 1804;[1] he had also taken, in 1804–1806, the Grand Tour of Europe. Washington's oldest brother William (Paulding's brother-in-law), who joined them after the first number as the versifier in the project, was forty-eight and a prominent New York merchant. While thus certainly not mere "Boys," these three, nevertheless, possessed a vivacity and wit that gave *Salmagundi* a youthful tone.

Their publisher David Longworth, nicknamed "Dusky Davy," almost equaled his authors in wit and whimsy. While taking pride in the elegance and correctness of the collections of belle lettres he printed, he took a lighthearted approach to his more lucrative task of publishing the official New York City directories, spicing this dry fare with self-ironic jokes and doggerel when the spirit moved him. He called his shop in Park Row near the theater "The Sentimental Epicure's Ordinary," and after his death in 1838, Paulding fondly recalled the "excellent hot cakes, the which he dispensed So liberally in his little Back room" (*Letters*, 222).[2]

Conceived, written, and printed in high spirits, the first number of *Salmagundi* appeared in the form of a yellow-backed, thirty-page pamphlet so small it could "be carried in old ladies' pockets and young ladies' work bags."[3] In their opening Advertisement, the anonymous authors facetiously declare their intention "to instruct the young, reform the old, correct the town and castigate the age" (67). They insist they will "have nothing to do with the pecuniary concerns of the paper" (68), and their publisher in his Notice professes "the same sublime contempt for money as his authors" (69) (which would prove to be quite false).

In the first number, the three controlling personae of the series make their appearance. Launcelot Langstaff, a mercurial old bachelor, apparently Paulding's creation, presides over the introductory essay from his "Elbow-Chair," assigning Anthony Evergreen the fashion department, because of his long experience "in the routine of balls, tea-parties, and assemblies," and appointing Will Wizard to the criticism department, because he has "had an opportunity of seeing the best singing girls, and tragedians of China" (70–71). Langstaff, maintaining a cocky and carefree tone, informs their readers that the size and time of appearance of the paper will vary; "This will best suit our negligent habits, and leave us that full liberty and independence which is the joy and pride of our souls" (73). In the second essay, "Theatrics," Wizard humorously discusses a recent New York performance of *Macbeth*, and Evergreen in "New York Assembly" concludes the number by poking fun at rival queens of fashion, the current dancing mania, and dancing Frenchmen.

The impudence and wit of *Salmagundi*'s first number gained it immediate attention, and, as Pierre M. Irving relates, "the sensation produced by it in the New York circles was intense, and great was the curiosity and speculation to know who were the mysterious trio, who, with such unquestioning confidence, had undertaken to amuse, edify, and castigate the town."[4] Encouraged by their success, the Salmagundians enlarged the scope of their work in subsequent numbers by creating other regular contributors. In No. 2, Langstaff's cousin Pindar Cockloft, a crotchety, fifty-eight-year-old bachelor of Cockloft Hall, who loves the past and hates the French, contributes the first of seven poems which playfully chide young belles on the errors of their ways. His first topic is their scanty fashions, which "give to each foppling that offers his hand, / Like Moses from Pisgah—a peep at the land" (86); later poems continue in this vein with warnings against the seductive verses of Thomas Moore, the pretensions of foplings, and the destructiveness of tea-table gossip.

In No. 3, Mustapha Rub-a-Dub Keli Khan, recently a prisoner in New York, supplies the first of nine letters to his kinsman in Tripoli, reporting a foreigner's impressions of the social and political happenings in the city. American rowdiness, a military review, wrangling in Congress, the grand bashaw's (Jefferson's) little gunboat navy, a political election, a city assembly, all eventually catch his eye and provoke his haughty conservative sensibility. In No. 4, Jeremy Cockloft, a callow youth fresh out of college, imitates British travel-writers in the first of three extracts from his book in progress about his tours of strange places, i.e., New Jersey, Pennsylvania, and Broadway. Meanwhile, Langstaff, Wizard, and Evergreen, the three old bachelors of

Cockloft Hall, continue to satirize the events, personalities, and opinions of Knickerbocker society, paying more than a little attention to what the town is saying about them.

The Fessenden Episode. An unusual feature of *Salmagundi* was the important role played by its readers in shaping the material included. The Salmagundians alluded often to individuals stung by their barbs or outraged by their impudence, and although many of these people were purely fictitious, some were quite real. Thomas Green Fessenden, comic versifier and editor of the *Weekly Inspector*, a political periodical, was one of the latter, and their exchange with him formed the most spirited episode in their project. In the February 7, 1808, issue of his paper, Fessenden sarcastically noticed the "new literary publication" and questioned its authors' supposed indifference to money.[5] In their third number of February 13, the Salmagundians congratulated themselves on having attracted the notice "of a ponderous genius of this city, Dr. Christopher Costive, L. L. D. &c." (Fessenden's bulk was distinctive) and promised "to serve him up a plentiful dish of flummery from his own shop, whenever he thinks fit to demand it, and garnished with a little Salmagundi for sauce" (97, 98).

Two weeks later, Fessenden took up the gauntlet in his *Inspector* article "SALMAGUNDI—*alias* BUBBLE AND SQUEAK—again." After ridiculing the "frothy productions" of the Salmagundians and claiming that "This sorry set of silly shoats, / Should be employed to milk *he-goats*," he unkindly pointed out the derivative nature of their efforts: " 'Whimwhams' is taken by this junto of notables from an English publication. Launcelot Langstaff is a vile daub of a caricature of Isaac Bickerstaff. Will Honeycomb sat for Anthony Evergreen; Will Wizard's original may be found in the British classics; and, in short, the prototype of every other character, with the exception of a few scurrilous personalities. The work ought to have been styled *Silly-kickaby*, alias *Taglocks of common English Publications*, compiled by Dunderpate, Doughhead, Dumpling and Co., published by Peter Pettyman. . . ."[6]

As one critic has pointed out, "This may have been true, but it was foolish to say so."[7] In reply, on February 24 the Salmagundians cooked *The Inspector*'s goose and kicked its ass in the poem "Flummery," which concluded:

This man as big as an elephant.
This *sweetest* witling of the age,
This hero, hangman, critic, sage,
This poet of five hundred pound
Has come to grace our hapless town.
And when he entered, every goose
Began to cackle like the deuce;
The asses brayed to one another—
Twas plain—the creatures smelt a brother.

(109)

Some seven pages of notes accompanied the poem, heaping additional abuse on Fessenden's size and the "quaintness, cuteness, and clumsiness" of his writings. After firing some harmless parting shots at the "lilliputian journal," in his issue for March 6, Fessenden left the Salmagundians alone.[8]

Although he erred in attacking *Salmagundi*, Fessenden accurately targeted its weakest spot: a heavy indebtedness to British examples, particularly the works of Addison and Goldsmith. From the *Spectator*, Paulding and the Irvings borrowed the idea of a club of eccentrics satirizing the follies of society, while from *The Citizen of the World*, they took the notion of satirizing local customs by having a foreigner describe them.[9] Swift and Rabelais were probably strong secondary influences as were two American periodicals, Joseph Dennie's *Port Folio* (1801–09) and Charles Brockden Brown's *Literary Magazine, and American Register* (1803–07).[10] In form and tone, then, *Salmagundi* was no foundling, but on the other hand, as the authors gained confidence in themselves and their abilities, it also proved to be no effete offspring.

Lines of Development. To its conclusion *Salmagundi*, as its name implied, remained a mixed dish of "Elbow-Chair" irony, comic verse, burlesque travel journals, caricatures of the Cockloft family, and satires on fashion, theaters, and New York politics; however, gradually the tone and content of *Salmagundi* became more serious and at times more artful as the work continued on into the spring, summer, and fall of 1807. Both Irving and Paulding contributed to this development, but they apparently did so in distinctly different ways.

The problem of *Salmagundi*'s authorship has been particularly difficult to solve because of the work's collaborative nature. In his

Preface to the 1835 Harpers edition, Paulding stated: "The thoughts of the authors were so mingled together in these essays, and they were so literally joint productions, that it would be difficult, as well as useless, at this distance of time, to assign to each his exact share." Bruce I. Granger, however, drawing upon six sets of attributions from various sources, including Paulding's own penciled notations of assignments he made in a presentation copy of the book, has assembled the most complete and reliable list of attributions to date.

According to Granger, Paulding wrote, or had the major hand in writing, the Publisher's Notice and Elbow-Chair essay in No. 1, "Mr. Wilson's Concert," "Character of Pindar Cockloft," and "Advertisement" in No. 2, the Mustapha letter, "Wise Conjectures of the Town," and possibly "*—How now mooncalf!*" in No. 3, "The Stranger in New Jersey" in No. 4, "Notes, by William Wizard" in No. 7, "Letter from Demy Semiquaver" in No. 10, "Mine Uncle John" in No. 11, the Elbow-Chair essay and "The Stranger at Home" in No. 12, probably "A Retrospect" in No. 13, "Sketches from Nature" in No. 15, "Style at Ballston" in No. 16, "Autumnal Reflections" in No. 17, the Mustapha letter in No. 18, probably the Anthony Evergreen essay in No. 19, and probably the Elbow-Chair essay in No. 20.[11]

This list, and Granger's similar lists for Irving and his brother William, reveal that it was Irving whose contributions first showed evidence that the Salmagundians had begun to take themselves and their work more seriously. In his essay "Answer to Certain Meddling Correspondents," appearing in No. 8 for April 18, he ill-humoredly compares their detractors to "those little yelping curs that infest our city, and who never fail to sally out and growl, and bark, and snarl" (162). After declaring, "we have resolved never to apologize," he self-righteously concludes, "*Good-nature* is our steersman, *reason* our ballast, *whim* the breeze that wafts us along, and MORALITY our leading star" (163, 164).

A month and a half later in No. 11, Irving again displayed little gentleness or whimsy in the letter from Mustapha, a strong, vicious condemnation of the democratic system. Mustapha, who in earlier letters had ridiculed Jefferson's red breeches and windy speeches, tells his kinsman that he has "seen that great political puppet-show—AN ELECTION," where the "buzzards of the party scamper from poll to poll" courting the *mother mob*, "the most pestilent, cross, crabbed, scolding, thieving, scratching, toping, wrongheaded, rebellious, and abominable termagant that ever was let loose in the world" (190–94). Although the words are Mustapha's, the sentiments are Irving's. As Stanley T. Williams has pointed out, "the young Federalist, lover of monarchies, held his nose at the sweaty nightcaps of American mobs. He could not endure readily the bungling maneuvers in the city streets of untrained soldiers, the beer-barrel orators, the gluttony and guzzling at two-penny national *fêtes.* Politically, Irving held the conservative corner in Dusky Davy's shop, and Paulding and William Irving apparently let him ride full course. He hurried on, occasionally beyond the borders of good humor. Jefferson he sometimes longed to obliterate."[12] In the essay "On Greatness" in No. 15 and the Mustapha letter of No. 16, Irving continued to bear down upon "the swinish multitude," but in the last Mustapha letter of No. 19, he turned from politics back to the social scene and wrote a charming, witty account of a city assembly and the bewitching young ladies in attendance.

Just as Irving became periodically less whimsical as the series progressed, Paulding did too, but in a more genial manner. He began to try his hand at the sustained personal essay, and three of his contributions, "Mine Uncle John" of No. 11, "A Retrospect" of No. 13, and "Autumnal Reflections" of No. 17, are mellow, polished pieces displaying a thoughtfulness and artistry absent in *Salmagundi*'s earlier numbers. The first, based on Paulding's actual Uncle John, combines descriptions of nature, small dramatic scenes complete with dialogue and action, and various reflections on his uncle's life, to paint a realistic, humorous, and slightly sentimental portrait of the old gentleman. Paulding's narrator, Langstaff, begins by saying that in spring "a thousand endearing recollections, forgotten amidst the cold pleasures and midnight dissipations of winter, arise to our remembrance" (196). He then recalls the last time he saw his uncle, fifteen years previously, during a visit to his old farm, where Langstaff lived as a schoolboy. His uncle, determined to show off his improvements, laughingly led him through bushes, briars, and hedges, eventually showing him his new stone fence, his invented cart, and his prize bull. After dinner, they went trout fishing as they had in the past, walking through familiar haunts and talking about past adventures, until "at length the shadows began to lengthen, the south-wind gradually settled into a perfect calm, and the sun threw his rays through the trees on the hill-top, in golden lustre, and a kind of sabbath stillness pervaded the whole valley" (197).

As the sun set, the old man talked about not fearing death, adding, "but still, when I pass such a day as this and contemplate such a scene, I cannot help feeling a latent wish to linger yet a little longer in this peaceful asylum, to enjoy a little more sunshine in this world, and to have a few more fishing matches with my boy" (198). He then prophetically "raised his hand a little from the fallen tree, and dropping it languidly by his side, turned himself towards home" (198). In the remainder of the essay, Langstaff explains how his uncle, whom he never saw again alive, had spent his life not doing things in too great a hurry and how he never married for he invariably lost whomever he courted to some "harum-scarum young fellow." Although unsophisticated compared to a similarly conceived modern essay such as E. B. White's "Once More to the Lake," "Mine Uncle John" possesses a poignancy and fidelity to life that save it from being ephemeral.

"A Retrospect," one of the most witty and polished pieces in the series, contains a similar nostalgic note, as Langstaff sadly reviews the results of the authors' efforts in the first volume. Mock seriousness is the dominant tone, however, as he self-ironically contrasts his past expectations with the present reality. "To a moral writer like myself," he declares, "who, next to his own comfort and entertainment, has the good of his fellow-citizens at heart, a retrospect is but a sorry amusement" (225). The reason? He expected "long ere this to have seen a complete reformation in manners and morals, atchieved [*sic*] by our united efforts" (225). Instead, "after all our lectures, precepts, and excellent admonitions, the people of New-York are nearly as much given to backsliding and ill-nature as ever; they are just as much abandoned to dancing and tea-drinking" (225). Scandal, according to Will Wizard's information, is rampant, the punning epidemic still rages, and what is worse, "the ladies still labour under the same scarcity of muslins, and delight in flesh-coloured silk stockings" (225).

These are sore disappointments, Langstaff says, and the authors are beginning "to suspect that many people read our numbers, merely for their amusement, without paying any attention to the serious truths conveyed in every page" (227). The authors comfort themselves, however, "by the reflection, that there are, at least, three good men left in this degenerate age, to benefit the world by example, should precept ultimately fail" (227). Additional solace comes from the perception that at least a few of their admonitions have been heeded. The young ladies, for example, have "not once indulged in that intoxicating, inflammatory, and whirligig dance, the *waltz*—ever since hot weather commenced" (228). In conclusion he recalls the authors' own "lingering moments of listless indifference and heavy-hearted despondency" and half-seriously declares: "We look back with delight upon many of these moments of mental gloom, whiled away by the cheerful exercise of our pen, and consider every such triumph over the spleen, as retarding the furrowing hand of time, in its insidious encroachments on our brows" (229). In this essay, Paulding achieves a consistently ironic blend of self-satire and social satire, with no lumps of ridiculousness or sarcasm showing through. The trick with this kind of humor, as Samuel Clemens would learn, is to motivate one's audience to laugh at the author's persona and at themselves, with the dignity of neither being damaged in the process. Here Paulding plays it well.

"Autumnal Reflections," Paulding's third nostalgic personal essay, deals with the stale topic of the relationship between autumn and old age; the piece is redeemed from triteness, however, by being metaphorically rich and thematically varied. Langstaff begins by reflecting on the evening of a man's life and how it shall end. "If haply his heart," he writes, "has escaped uninjured through the dangers of a seductive world, it may then administer to the purest of his felicities, and its chords vibrate more musically for the trials they have sustained—like the viol, which yields a melody sweet in proportion to its age" (266). After describing the progress of the seasons in the woods near his home at Cockloft Hall, he draws a connection between "the feelings of the aged with the decline of the year" (268). He admits, however, that his old Cousin Pindar "still possesses much of the fire and energy of youthful sentiment" (268) and does not blend into the scheme. Pindar thus inspires Langstaff to reflect that "when I see a hale, hearty old man, who has jostled through the rough path of the world, without having worn away the fine edge of his feelings, or blunted his sensibility to natural and moral beauty, I compare him to the evergreen of the forest, whose colours, instead of fading at the approach of winter, seem to assume additional lustre, when contrasted with the surrounding desolation" (269).

Langstaff concludes his set piece by describing an afternoon stroll taken in the company of Pindar to the top of a high hill at sunset. Although Langstaff's reflections are melancholy, he lets Pindar have the last word with the statement that "though the spring is past, the summer over, and the autumn come—still you and I go on our way rejoicing—and while, like the lofty mountains of our Southern America, our heads are covered with snow, still, like them, we feel the genial warmth of spring and summer playing upon our bosoms" (269).

Although all three of these essays lack depth and originality, they show, in their handling of character, setting, and tone, signs of a promising creative writer at work. Irving's best essays in the series, "Chronicles of the City of Gotham" of No. 17 and "The Little Man in Black" of No. 18, are likewise lightweight and conventional, yet indicative of better work to come. One critic has pointed out that "on these more self-respecting essays [of Paulding and Irving] rests the only hope of *Salmagundi* to be known as a corner of American literature."[13] Few consider it such, but many might if the series had continued and thus profited from the authors' rapidly developing talents. Although neither Paulding nor the Irvings wished to conclude the project, they did so out of disenchantment with Longworth's commercialism. He raised the price of the work to a shilling, took out a copyright after they chose not to, and, according to Paulding, "declined to concede to us a share of the profits which had become very considerable, and the work was abruptly discontinued."[14]

***Salmagundi's* Popularity.** The profits Paulding refers to arose from *Salmagundi*'s remarkable contemporary popularity. With each number it gained new readers, and, according to Pierre M. Irving, a record eight-hundred copies were once sold in one day.[15] Eventually its circulation extended to other American cities where soon appeared shortlived imitations, which lacked its sophistication and easy fit into the lives of fashionable Americans. In 1819 Richard H. Dana recalled, "It was exceedingly pleasant morning or after-dinner reading, never taking up too much of a gentleman's time from his business and pleasures, nor so exalted and spiritualized as to seem mystical to his far reaching vision. It was an excellent thing in the rests between cotillions, and pauses between games at cards."[16]

Trite, trivial, vicious though it was in parts, *Salmagundi* as a whole displayed exceptionable staying power and earned its authors national and international recognition. In 1810 John Lambert, an English traveler who would publish the book in London, predicted that "as a correct picture of the people of New York, and other parts of the country, . . . it will always be read with interest by a native of the United States."[17] He could have added "and by some foreigners as well" and still have been right, for by 1902, it had passed through at least thirty-four editions—nineteen American, thirteen English, one French, and one Swedish.[18]

In 1860 William Cullen Bryant aptly summarized the attributes, other than historical interest, that give *Salmagundi* its enduring appeal:

> Its gayety is its own; its style of humor is not that of Addison nor Goldsmith, though it has all the genial spirit of theirs; nor is it borrowed from any other writer. It is far more frolicsome and joyous, yet tempered by a native gracefulness. "Salmagundi" was manifestly written without the fear of criticism before the eyes of the authors, and to this sense of perfect freedom, in the exercise of their genius, the charm is probably owing, which makes us still read it with so much delight. Irving never seemed to place much value on the part he contributed to this work, yet I doubt whether he ever excelled some of those papers in Salmagundi, which bear the most evident marks of his style; and Paulding, though he has since acquired a reputation by his other writings, can hardly be said to have written any thing better, than the best of those which are ascribed to his pen.[19]

Although slightly too generous, Bryant's estimate of *Salmagundi* is sound.

Irving and Paulding. Ironically, Irving, as Bryant indicates, became one of *Salmagundi*'s chief detractors. In 1819 he wrote Brevoort that "the work was pardonable as a juvenile production, and has been indulgently received by the public. But it is full of errors, puerilities & impertinences. . . . I was in hopes it would gradually have gone down into oblivion."[20] Some thirty years later, he continued to be embarrassed by it and refused to include it in the revised edition of his writings (1848–1851).

Paulding, on the other hand, defended *Salmagundi* in letters to Irving and proudly included it in his own collected works of 1835. In 1824 he wrote Irving, "I don't hold this early bantling of ours in such utter contempt as you do, and can't help viewing it in the light of a careless popular thing that will always be read in spite of its faults, perhaps in consequence of these very faults" (*Letters*, 70). Nine years later, he reiterated these sentiments to Irving, and in materials his son quoted in the 1867 *Literary Life*, Paulding may again have had Irving in mind when he called *Salmagundi* "one of those productions of youth that wise men—or those who think themselves wise—are very apt to be ashamed of when they grow old."[21]

If one assumes, as more than one uninformed critic has, that *Salmagundi*'s merits resulted from Irving's genius and its faults from his collaborators' deficiencies,[22] then Irving's attitude can be interpreted as irritation at those on his coattails and Paulding's as unbecoming desire for a free ride. Such a view, however, lacks truth and fairness. The work's most unattractive feature, the vicious political satire directed at President Jefferson and republicanism, almost certainly flowed from Irving's pen, and at least three of the most appealing and sophisticated essays in the series came from Paulding's; thus, the contempt and fondness of the two were probably inspired by their own writings, respectively.

The revisions Irving made in a subsequent edition of the work confirm that he indeed saw the political satire as its most pervasive fault, and Paulding's later revisions indicate that he did as well. For the Paris edition of 1824, Irving excised numerous political references, particularly those directed at Jefferson. A slur on his gunboat policy, the rumor that he kept a black mistress, and passages critical of logocracy, economy, and mobocracy, were either omitted or revised.[23] Similarly, he toned down the essay "On Greatness," tentatively assigned to him, which dealt with the great politician created by "the swinish multitude."[24] (The Fessenden material had already been removed by David Longworth in the 1814 New York edition, which Irving used as his copy-text.)[25]

Likewise Paulding, for the 1835 Harpers edition, based on Irving's revised Paris one, further moderated the political satire, replacing Irving's Mustapha letter of No. 11, satirizing a city election, with a new letter of his own describing the impressive order that coexists with liberty. Similarly, he replaced the essay "On Greatness" with a gentler satiric piece about a gentleman who married four times and each time discovered his mistake. Paulding also deleted slighting references to Thomas Paine and Thomas Jefferson that Irving had left in.[26]

Because of Paulding's embittered contributions to the Paper War with England and the amiability of Irving's subsequent works, critics have misinterpreted the nature of their contributions to *Salmagundi.* In 1825 John Neal, writing in *Blackwood's Magazine*, declared that "the papers of Paulding are more sarcastic, ill-natured, acrimonious—bitter, than those of Irving; but quite as able." One month later he added, "No two writers could be more thoroughly opposed, in everything—disposition—habit—style—than were Irving and Paulding. The former was cheerful; pleasant; given to laughing at whatever he saw—not peevishly—satirically or spitefully—but in real good humour: the latter—even while he *laughed*—as Byron says of Lara—*sneered.* Irving would make us love human nature—wish it well—or pity it: Paulding would make us ashamed of it; or angry with it. One looks for what is good—in everything; the other, for what is bad."[27] According to one editor of the 1977 definitive edition of *Salmagundi*, these observations of Neal display acumen.[28] In fact, they do not, but others have repeated them in various forms over the years nevertheless.

One of the few readers accurately to assess Paulding's contribution to the work was Evert A. Duyckinck, the highly respected and gifted editor of the *Literary World* (1847–53). In his Preface to the 1860 edition of *Salmagundi*, Duyckinck gives Paulding credit for writing "a considerable portion of the book," attributing to him "many of the exquisite passages of description of nature," "Mine Uncle John," which he calls "a mellow, fine toned portrait," and "Autumnal Reflections," "one of the most refined sentimental papers of the volume." Duyckinck then adds: "It is, perhaps, a common misapprehension of this eminent writer, that his pen was wanting in geniality, and that he took rather a splenetic view of life. This notion has probably arisen from the admission of a controversial element into his productions where, perhaps, it might have been better shut out; but certainly, with this exception, no American writer has spread upon his page more feeling observation, more friendly truths, more genial sympathies."[29]

Unfortunately, however, Duyckinck's is a minority report. Paulding's collaboration with Irving in *Salmagundi* eventually injured his reputation irreparably by giving his many political and literary assailants a heavy club with which to brutalize him. One of his nastiest beatings came at the hands of N. P. Willis, a vain, social-climbing New York editor, writer, and dandy, who thought Paulding, then Secretary of the Navy, had socially slighted him.[30] In an 1839 review of Paulding's collected works, Willis wrote:

> Every lion has his jackal. Paulding was Washington Irving's. . . . Mr. Paulding had furnished the alloy to Irving's gold in Salmagundi, and they fancied that if the fusion could be continued a while, he might *pass*, alone. . . . The one rule was, *never separate their names*. Irving and Paulding! *Irving and Paulding*! IRVING AND PAULDING! Every old maid on the Hudson took the slogan like an echo. . . . Irving had consented to write in the same book with him. All the newspapers echoed the union. The public took it for granted they were linked for immortality. Who were the principal American authors? "Irving and Paulding!" Who wrote Salmagundi? "Irving and Paulding!" Who wrote the Sketch-book? "Irving and Paulding!" The words stuck together, from constant repetition, like the names of a mercantile firm. . . . He hung on to good Geoffrey's skirts like a shadow. . . . The echo, however, did not reach John Bull's ears. John Bull cried out for "Irving," but the jackal strained his ears in vain for the appendage. . . . We are glad that our great and beloved author, Washington Irving, has at last followed the example of Peter Schlemihl, and *sold his shadow*. . . . Out he went like a candle snuff—one day Paulding and Irving—the next, Paulding the ship-chandler. One day half an author at least—the next, a patient old gentleman cyphering his way to a secretaryship. There he sits—all honor to his new dignity![31]

Although no subsequent critic of Paulding's works has displayed Willis's cruelty, many have followed his lead, some even borrowing his derogatory imagery. In 1935, for example, Fred Lewis Pattee wrote that Paulding followed Irving "like a veritable shadow," adding that he completely lacked "Irving's leading asset: mellow atmospheres and that glow of genial sunniness for which there is no critical name save Washington Irving." Similarly, in 1944 Van Wyck Brooks called Paulding "a shadow and understudy of Irving," and one "whose glory it was to have worked with Irving."[32]

To his credit, Irving privately defended Paulding from such invidious comparisons. In 1820 he lauded the "truth and beauty" of Paulding's writings in a letter to Brevoort and declared, "It is an ungenerous and unkind thing to put him and me in contrast . . . and to praise me at his expense. . . . I neither deserve, nor desire distinction of that kind and those that make it, do not understand our distinct and comparative merit."[33]

Paulding, to his credit also, never spoke slightingly of Irving or blamed him for the unfairness *Salmagundi* engendered. The closest he came was to tell Rufus Griswold in 1846 that "my Countrymen have done me great injustice, in assigning the work to Mr. Irving alone" (*Letters*, 426). For the most part Paulding took pride in Irving's successes and offered him encouragement whenever he needed it. In 1825, for example, after a host of American and English reviewers attacked Irving's *Tales of a Traveller* (1824) and accused him of plagiarism, effeminacy, and sycophancy, Paulding wrote his deeply distressed friend: "Whatever little rubs of this kind you may receive, place them to the account of the spleen and envy of unsuccessful rivals. . . . As to the voice of your own country, it is entirely in your favor. She is proud of you, and the most obscure recesses of the land, even old Sleepy Hollow, are becoming almost classical, in consequence of the notice you have taken of them. . . . You know that I am rather a cynic than a flatterer, and you ought to know that of all men I would not flatter you." Paulding poignantly concluded, "Farewell my dear Washington—though you are not building houses like Brevoort, or villages like unto Gouv [Gouverneur Kemble], you are building what will last longer than either. God bless you" (*Letters*, 82–83).

Paulding was right, of course, about "The Legend of Sleepy Hollow" at least, as any current anthology of American literature will attest. Paulding's own reputation, however, while reaching a considerable height by the mid-1830s, eventually declined, in part due to the inescapable comparisons with Irving, whose reputation revived and thrived on into the last half of the nineteenth century. Without *Salmagundi*, however, both men might never have achieved the stature that they did. Because of its success, the work inspired them to pursue their literary interests, and it established the satiric tone of many of their subsequent writings. Perhaps more importantly, it also inaugurated a tradition of humor (later termed Knickerbocker humor) that vitalized the New York literary scene for more than fifty years. Taken from eighteenth-century English quarters, *Salmagundi*'s satiric, Rabelasian spirit became naturalized in nineteenth-century America, and as late as 1851 one native New Yorker eagerly adopted it in the opening chapters of one of America's greatest books, *Moby-Dick.*[34]

Salmagundi, Second Series

In the spring of 1819, Paulding, at the instigation of his Philadelphia publisher, Moses Thomas, undertook on his own the continuation of *Salmagundi.* His timing could not have been worse. Some twelve years had elapsed since the first series delighted New Yorkers, and Paulding was now a recently married, forty-year-old secretary of the Board of Navy Commissioners living in Washington. As such, he lacked the youthful vivacity and intimate knowledge of New York society so necessary to the success of the earlier series; furthermore, the diverse, cosmopolitan, business-minded population of that city, now 50 percent larger, had outgrown its interest in the whim-whams and opinions of Launcelot Langstaff. To make matters worse, at the same time Paulding began the project, Washington Irving initiated his own periodical series, *The Sketch Book*, which, written with much care and labor, contained his finest work and captivated audiences in both the United States and England.

Irving's first number, sent from London on March 3, 1819, appeared in the United States in mid-May; Paulding's first number appeared two weeks later on May 30. This head-to-head competition, lasting for a year and a half, was purely coincidental. In a January 1820 letter to Irving, Paulding explained, ". . . until Gouv. Kemble brought your first number down to Washington with him, I was entirely ignorant that you contemplated any thing of the kind. But for an accidental delay, my first No. would have got the start of yours. As it happened however, it had the appearance of taking the field against you, a thing which neither my head nor heart will sanction. I believe my work has not done you any harm in the way of rivalship, for it has been soundly abused by many persons, and compared with the first part with many degrading expressions" (*Letters*, 61). Paulding's comments on the effects of the rivalry are here understated, for twenty-six years later he more candidly explained that "it so happened that the first number [of *Salmagundi, Second Series*] came out about the same time with [Mr. Irving's] Crayon Sketches, which swallowed me up at one gulp" (*Letters*, 426).

Salmagundi, Second Series ran through fifteen numbers, which appeared monthly, with the exception of a hiatus during March-June 1820, and it concluded on September 2, 1820.[35] No. 1 contains four pieces, which are longer and better written, yet less lively and whimsical, than those in the first series. In the Introduction Langstaff nostalgically observes that little remains "of the circle we last parted with, but the remembrance of a pleasant, long-past dream" (1:12). He relates that he, Evergreen, and Wizard are still single and still "enjoy the delights of unrestrained freedom in this unequalled town" (1:12), admitting nonetheless, "I am somewhat graver than I was; but whether wiser or not, must be left to the judgment of the public" (1:13). In the Elbow-Chair essay, Langstaff rather moralistically satirizes Mr. Tubman, one of the noveau riche, and his gaudily furnished home. In "Codification" Wizard then humorously lists some still-familiar rules of fashionable behavior that require the ladies to wear little, talk loudly, and flirt with married men, and the men to ignore their spouses, spend money, and act young. The last essay, "Criticism," is a parody in which Geoffrey Cockloft, a fictitious contemporary critic, writes a convincingly abusive review of *Othello* and advises its young author to give up playwriting for which he obviously has no talent.

Although this first number was competent and witty, Paulding apparently became demoralized by the appearance of Irving's rival publication and the unfavorable reception of his own work, for in No. 2 through No. 5, he became progressively less inspired and humorous. In fact, the topics of death, sorrow, injustice, and madness began to pervade the series, and the tone, while at times striving toward gaiety and lightheartedness, became more brittle and grim.

No. 5 appeared on September 4, 1819, and when Brevoort wrote Irving on September 9, stating that Paulding "is making sad work of it," he was right. After explaining that Paulding had asked him "for hints for a paper on the subject of my whimsical old father," Brevoort added: "he seems resolved upon his literary suicide—in other words to destroy himself solely by his own means.—I am really astonished how he can possibly write so much below his natural capacity, and not perceive it."[36] Paulding probably did perceive it, but motivated no doubt by his stubborn sense of pride, he mushed on, eventually writing several respectable pieces and one brilliant one.

In No. 6, using Brevoort's "hints," he drew a fair sketch of a gentleman farmer devoted to his various fowls, which he rules over as a benevolent dictator; in the same number, "The Country Village" presents a strong and witty satire of a club of village gossips. With No. 7 Paulding continued to raise the quality of the series. The Elbow-Chair essay contains a thoughtful, well-written disquisition on the virtues of good taste and refinement, while "The Art of Living" skillfully directs social criticism against administrators of charities who line their own pockets at the expense of the poor. In No. 8, another respectable piece appeared, "The Old Ferry House," a short story about an old man whose daughter drowns in the Hudson during a storm as he anxiously waits in the Ferry House. A modicum of realism, local color, and pathos distinguishes the tale.

For overall quality No. 9 is the best of the series. It begins with a touching, well-drawn sketch of an old woman during the Revolution who loses her son at the hands of the Yagers and is comforted by General Washington; "Signs of the Times" is a durable piece of social criticism, dramatizing the evils of the state lotteries; and "Town and Country" contains a saucy, funny letter from a young flirt who calls herself Adiante, matched by another letter from a Virginian correspondent telling of his travels in the West and the hardships encountered by a pioneer from Connecticut.

With No. 10, Paulding forsook humor altogether and dealt acutely with serious social issues, namely, racial unrest, religious fanaticism, and paper money. Sometime in April of 1820, Brevoort informed Irving that "Paulding's Salmagundi died the death at the 10th Number,"[37] but he was mistaken, for after a three-month discontinuance, Paulding brought out No. 11 on July 8. This number and the next three, however, contain only borrowed or trifling material. For his last number, though, Paulding wrote a forceful essay "On the Influence of Foreign Literature" (omitted from subsequent editions) and a brilliant eight-page introduction to a story entitled "The Wreck of Genius." This introduction, retitled "National Literature" for subsequent editions, where it appears as a separate piece, has been the most often anthologized of all of Paulding's writings and rightfully so. It represents a major contribution to American literary nationalism, and, more importantly, it contains some of the most original and thoughtful statements about fiction writing to be found in nineteenth-century criticism. As will be discussed in chapter 5, Paulding's theory of "Rational Fictions" presented in this essay, when combined with the best of his other literary criticism, shows him to be if not "a genius, whose critical insight and analysis preceded his creative works," as Amos Herold has claimed,[38] at least a gifted literary theorist, whose critical abilities were unmatched by any of his American contemporaries.

Overall *Salmagundi, Second Series* contains much chaff, but its few grains of value make one glad Paulding wrote it. He was not unaware, of course, of its irritating unevenness, and the last essay of the last number contains a veiled plea for tolerance. After Anthony Evergreen announces that Langstaff has died and that his epitaph is not yet written, he concludes: "The reader may make one to please himself, provided he does not venture to insinuate that the old gentleman ought to have died some ten years ago" (2:300).

Chapter Three

Anti-British Satires

Paulding's Nationalism

Almost all readers agree that the most prominent characteristic of Paulding's writings is his nationalism. As Evert A. Duyckinck first pointed out, Paulding "found his inspiration at home at a time when American woods and fields, and American traits of society, were generally supposed to furnish little if any materials for originality. He not merely drew his nourishment from his native soil, but whenever 'that mother of a mighty race' was assailed from abroad by accumulated injuries and insults, stood up manfully in defence of her rights and her honor. He has never on any occasion bowed to the supremacy of European example or European criticism; he is a stern republican in all his writings."[1] Paulding's nationalism, as Duyckinck suggests, consisted of both positive and negative sentiments, love for America and hatred for her antagonists, particularly England.

His anglophobia stemmed in part from the lingering Dutch resentment of the British colonial occupation of New York and in part from the suffering of his family at the hands of the British during the Revolution. It was later strengthened by British actions before and during the War of 1812 and by the abuse heaped upon Americans by a number of British writers for fifty years following the Revolution.

Many Americans with republican sympathies, including Presidents Madison, Jackson, and Van Buren, responded appreciatively to Paulding's nationalism,[2] but some of his conservative contemporaries did not. His friends Brevoort and Irving, for example, viewed his hostility toward England with bemused condescension. In 1815 Irving wrote to Brevoort from France: "These late triumphs on the continent will be sore blows to Jim's plans—they will materially delay the great object of his life—the overthrow of the British Empire."[3] Some fifteen years later, Brevoort adopted the same tone when he observed in a letter to Irving that Cooper "and Paulding will never rest until they have laid that old sinner England upon her back, exposed to the derision of the whole world. It is an enterprise worthy of Don Quixotte [*sic*]."[4]

Paulding's nationalism, a creative tool as well as a destructive weapon, was always at hand as he wrote, and viewed in retrospect his efforts define him more accurately as a pioneer than a knight errant, for the adversities he faced—prejudice, disdain, abuse, self-doubt, and the stifling forces of tradition—were both real and powerful. Though often misdirected and mishandled, his nationalism ultimately served him well in his pioneering efforts, which took a variety of forms. In his literary criticism, discussed in chapter 5, his insistence that Amercan fiction and drama be national, original, and realistic was some fifty years ahead of its time; in his poetry, plays, short stories, and novels (discussed in chapters 4, 6, 7, and 8 respectively), he led the way in the use of American materials and themes; and in his anti-British satires (discussed in this chapter), he defended the United States with more sustained wit and vigor than any other writer of his day.

Paulding and the Paper War

During the first four decades of the nineteenth century, a number of American writers, with Paulding at the fore, fought a defensive battle of words with British travel-writers and reviewers who denigrated and distorted American manners and institutions.[5] During this period, most Americans felt particularly sensitive to criticism from abroad, for they lacked confidence in the successful outcome of their democratic experiment, and they recognized the obvious cultural inadequacies of their new nation; nevertheless, it was British jealousy and disdain, rather than American sensitivity, which provoked and sustained the controversy. At the turn of the century, many Englishmen, particularly those associated with the Tory government, still smarted from America's successful Revolution and her close ties with England's arch enemy, France; in the next decades they then had to endure the American independence and military victories of the War of 1812; and finally during the 1820s and 1830s, they resented the United States' attraction of British emigrants and her influence on the growing republican spirit of the English masses, which led to the Chartist uprisings and the Reform Bill of 1832.

The Beginnings. Of the early British travel-writers, few dealt harshly with the America they encountered. As Allan Nevins has pointed out, from 1788 to about 1825, the British traveler came to the United States for "utilitarian inquiry." He visited to ascertain this country's potentialities as a field for investment or for beginning a professional career. "Most of the travellers came over hopefully and returned with their hopes confirmed."[6] A handful of travelers, however, such as Isaac Weld, William Cobbett, Charles William Janson, and Thomas Ashe, returned with ill will or frustration and wrote unfavorable and untruthful accounts of life in America.

The first American writers to respond to and satirize this breed of British writer were Paulding and Irving.[7] In the fourth number of *Salmagundi*, published February 24, 1807, Irving used the Elbow-Chair essay to criticize "travel mongers" and with the first installment of Jeremy Cockloft's travel diary, which followed, Paulding parodied several of them. Jeremy's "Memorandums for a Tour, to be entitled 'The Stranger in New-Jersey; or Cockney Travelling' " includes the following notes: "Princeton . . . mem. American students very much addicted to burning down colleges—reminds me of a good story, nothing at all to the purpose . . . Left Princeton . . . stage-driver took a *swig*—mem. set down all the people as drunkards— . . . Trenton—attempted to kiss the chamber maid—boxed my ears till they rung like our theatre bell—girl had lost one tooth—mem. all the American ladies prudes, and have bad teeth" (103–6).

In No. 12 of *Salmagundi*, Paulding again ridiculed the English traveler with his account of Tom Straddle, a cockney from Birmingham, who "had been splashed half a dozen times by the carriages of nobility" and "could, therefore, talk of nobility and despise the untitled plebians of America" (202). Sent by his employers as an agent to America, Tom "considered himself as going among a nation of barbarians, where he would be received as a prodigy" (203). Having heard of the beauty of American women, he "put good store of beads, spike-nails, and looking glasses in his trunk to win the affections of the fair ones, as they paddled about in their bark canoes" (203). Although ignored on his arrival, Tom "bought horses and equipages" and "became quite a man of *ton*" (204), criticizing all things American. Eventually, however, his creditors rose in rebellion against him, and he went "*smash* like a hero" (206).

This light-hearted satire in *Salmagundi* apparently went unnoticed in England, for two years later, in November 1809, the newly established *Quarterly Review* published a vicious attack on American manners, insisting that "there is . . . both in the physical and intellectual features of the Americans a trace of savage character."

Quite possibly inspired by this review, Paulding began writing several years later his play *The Bucktails* (discussed in chapter 6), which was not published until 1847. The plot revolves around the visit to England of two American gentlemen, Henry and Frank Tudor. Their English hosts, Mr. Obsolete and his sister, dread their arrival; "Lord, brother, what shall we do with these aboriginals?" Miss Obsolete asks. "I have been assured they wear copper rings in their noses—eat raw meat—paint one-half their faces red and the other black—and are positively half naked."[8] The Tudors, of course, prove to be gentlemen of the best sort, and earn the respect and affection of all.

When *The Quarterly* joined forces with those British travelers who regarded Americans as savages, the war of words between the two countries intensified. One of the most consequential defenses in America appeared in 1810 when C. Jared Ingersoll, a native Philadelphian assuming the guise of an Irish Jesuit visiting America, published a brief and moderate volume entitled *Inchiquin, The Jesuit's Letters.* Two years later, Paulding joined the Paper War with his first book, *The Diverting History of John Bull and Brother Jonathan,* a humorous satire (discussed in detail below), and in 1813, under the influence of ill will generated by the War of 1812, he then fired a stronger volley at Britain with his book-length poem, *The Lay of the Scottish Fiddle* (discussed in chapter 4), which parodied Sir Walter Scott and satirized, rather indignantly, the British military actions on the Chesapeake.

Paulding's *Lay* and *Inchiquin's Letters* were reviewed by the *Quarterly* in its January 1814 number and used as an excuse for launching the most virulent assaults to date on the American people. The reviewer of *Inchiquin's Letters* conducts what he calls an "inquiry" into the character of the American people. Looking at the present generation of politicians, he finds that "In America the 'man of the people' is one who frequents the grog-shops, smokes his segar and harangues the populace with violent and inflammatory abuse of the hostile faction"; members of Congress "actually spit at, and kick each other"; and even judges engage in boxing matches, resulting in black eyes for the losers. Turning to the manners of the people, he sees other barbarities including the inquisitiveness of Americans, the rudeness of tavern keepers, and the practice of bundling at taverns where an assortment of travelers "retire into one common chamber, with as many beds in it as an hospital-ward, into which they bundle promiscuously in pairs between dirty sheets that are washed once in three months." In America, nuptial vows are disregarded, he observes; negro slaves "are bought, sold, bartered, hard worked, ill fed, flogged with cow skins," and "dram-drinking and its sister grace tobacco-smoking . . . seem to pervade all ages and conditions." Gouging, kicking, and biting also occur frequently, he claims, adding that "Janson actually saw a crowd applauding a fellow while he held up his antagonist's eye in his hand" and Ashe found that " 'In *roughing and tumbling*, it is *allowable* to *peel* the skull, tear out the eyes, and *smooth away* the nose.' "[9]

This ungenerous review achieved instant notoriety in America and inspired Paulding's *The United States and England*, a restrained argumentative treatise that tried to refute the *Quarterly*'s charges by showing that its sources were unreliable, its generalizations based on insufficient evidence, and its fault-finding methods more applicable to England than America. Paulding continued his battle against the *Quarterly* in his *Letters from the South* (1817). The two volumes are primarily discursive essays on the people and places he saw on his trip through Virginia in 1816, with various reflections injected at random; however, letter XXXIII contains a rather embittered, but accurate, evaluation of the *Quarterly* and its editor (William Gifford), certainly one of the most hateful literary critics of his or any time. Paulding relates that this editor "was once a cabin-boy in a Newcastle Collier" and that "his ungovernable hostility to the Americans, arose from his having once been terrible flogged by a Yankey sailor at Wapping." As this boy rose in station with the help of "some munificent gentlemen," Paulding says, he "began to assume all the airs of a man of high aristocratic birth, tacked esquire to his name, and on all occasions expressed his utter contempt for democrats and common people." Now, as editor of the *Quarterly,* "his criticism partakes of that coarse harshness, which almost always distinguishes a low man, raised by fortune rather than merit, to a height he neither sustains by his dignity, nor adorns by his modest worth."[10]

Mid-War Developments. As Paulding was thus venting his anger at Gifford and the *Quarterly*, his friend Irving was in London becoming friends with the British literati, including Jeffrey, Moore, Campbell, and Scott, and he would soon win even Gifford's affection.[11] In the second number of his *Sketch Book*, Irving rebuked Paulding implicitly in "English Writers on America" asking, "What have we to do with national prejudices?" and advising, "Let it be the pride of our writers . . . discarding all feelings of irritation, and disdaining to retaliate the illiberality of British authors, to speak of the English nation without prejudice, and with determined candor."[12]

As Irving was sounding retreat for his countrymen, in England new offensives were launched in the Paper War. The *Quarterly* continued its campaign of abuse, which was soon supported by *Blackwood's Magazine* and occasionally the *Edinburgh Review.* In January 1820, the latter published Sydney Smith's famous article, which deeply offended by sneeringly asking: "In the four quarters of the globe, who reads an American book? or goes to an American play? or looks at an American picture or statue?"[13]

During the 1820s, Paulding, and later Cooper, defended the United States from these and similar attacks. In *Salmagundi, Second Series*, Paulding calmly analyzed the prejudices and pernicious influences of the *Edinburgh Review* and the *Quarterly* in a twenty-seven-page essay "On the Influence of Foreign Literature" that appeared in No. 15. He omitted this essay from subsequent editions of *Salmagundi, Second Series*, however, probably because much of its argument he incorporated into his next contribution to the Paper War, *A Sketch of Old England* (1822), a fake travel book, captious in content and tone.

A Sketch provoked a long, devastatingly mocking review in the *Quarterly* in January 1824, and this review in turn seems to have inspired Paulding's *John Bull in America* (1825), a very funny satire (discussed in detail below) aimed directly at British travelers and the *Quarterly.*

1825 to the End. Between 1825 and 1835, British travel books became increasingly more critical of American life and manners, with Captain Basil Hall's *Travels in North America in the Years 1827–28*

(1829) and Frances Trollope's *Domestic Manners of the Americans* (1832) inspiring the most ill will. Hall, a retired British naval officer who had turned to travel, study, and writing, came to America with High-Tory prejudices that colored his observations of American political life. Although his social comments were acute, the political portions of his book, which deplored various democratic practices, outraged Americans. In Volume II of *Westward Ho!* (1832), Paulding interrupted his narrative to rebut Hall, whom he caricatures as Mr. Bartram, an Englishman conducting "a close and minute investigation of the true state of the country, by riding through it as fast as a comet."[14] Bartram expresses the conviction that a system of equality is impossible, and when asked where he derived it, answers, "From England, sir, from my own country.... Why, sir, don't we every day see the consequences of the mob getting uppermost; destruction of property and lives?" (2:122). Paulding, through his protagonist, replies, "That is just because there is no equality among you, and not because there is. It is the sense of inequality, and its attendant wants and mortifications, that produce these violent eruptions of popular discontent" (2:122). For more than four pages, Paulding continued to knock down his straw likeness of Hall, undoubtedly to the cheers of his contemporary readers, and in the 1835 edition of *Diverting History*, he again thumped another likeness, "Captain All," for five pages, using ridicule to do so.

Mrs. Trollope, who shared Hall's High-Tory prejudices, was a pretentious snob whose impractical husband had failed as a lawyer and a farmer. She came to the United States in 1827 to invest in a business, and, after settling in the fast growing but rough western town of Cincinnati, opened a bazaar for the sale of fancy-goods and knick-knacks, which failed dismally. She blamed the vulgarity of Cincinnati society for her failure, and not surprisingly, her best-selling *Domestic Manners of the Americans* is thoroughly malicious and bitter, though also lively and readable.

In the year it appeared, it was condemned by numerous journals and newspapers throughout America, and during the next four years at least six books, including Paulding's 1835 edition of *Diverting History*, rebutted or satirized its author. Paulding also parodied her in the anonymous "Leaves from Mrs. Trollope's Journal" published in the *New-York Mirror* in the summer of 1832,[15] and several months later he revised his play *The Lion of the West* (discussed in chapter 6) so as to include the very funny caricature of her as Mrs. Wollope.

Although Charles Dickens's *American Notes* (1842) generated new controversy when it appeared, by the late 1830s the Paper War had lost its intensity and was to all intents and purposes over. Paulding, however, maintained enough interest in it to fire an inconsequential parting shot with his 1846 satiric essay "Peter Pettifog, the Great Traveller, and Id Genus Omne," which appeared in the *Columbian Magazine.*

Diverting History

Having gained an overview of the Paper War and Paulding's extensive participation in it, one can more clearly understand the reactionary elements in his two major anti-British satires: *The Diverting History of John Bull and Brother Jonathan* (1812) and *John Bull in America* (1825). The first was published under the pseudonym of Hector Bull-Us and written amid the tensions that would soon lead to the War of 1812. The book's sixteen brief chapters provide a humorous allegorical account of the relations between America and England from the colonial period up to the present, and conclude by satirizing New England's current opposition to President Madison and her reluctance to contribute funds for the war.

Paulding begins his "history" by describing an early quarrel between Squire Bull, "a cholerick old fellow, who held a good manor in the middle of a great mill pond,"[16] and his youngest son, Jonathan. The source of contention is the correct name for churches, and when the Squire makes life unbearable at home because of the quarrel, Jonathan paddles across the mill pond to some new lands "to which the Squire pretended some sort of claim" (2), there clearing the woods and laying out thirteen good farms. In a short time, the tall, shrewd, "broad-footed cub of a fellow" (3) prospers so well, that Bull grows "to be very fond of him" and undertakes "to pick his pockets" (1), but Jonathan bests the Squire in a scuffle and makes him give up all claim to the farms.

When Jonathan takes a wife [Congress], Mrs. Bull [Parliament] denounces her as an "illbred, illegitimate minx" (5) and quarrels with any neighbors who visit her. The Squire also harbors resentment toward his son and has his boatmen harass Jonathan's tenants when they fish or sail on the pond. As he progresses into his dotage, Bull imagines he owns the pond and decides he would like a slice of the manor of Frogmore [France] as well, which has recently been acquired by one Beau Napperty [Napoleon]. Affecting a liking for the late Louis Baboon [Louis XVI], Bull joins in an attempt to kick Napperty out of the manor, ostensibly to return it to the Baboon heirs, but during the ensuing scuffle, Bull's tenants are driven home, with Bull's overseer [William Pitt] assuring him it "was one of the most *brilliant affairs* that ever happened" (27). The Squire, as cocky as ever, then goes about righting the wrongs, as he calls it, of all of his neighbors, including Don Carlos [Charles IV] over at the Point [Spain], while Napperty continues upholding the rights of man, as he calls it, and "betwixt the two, the whole neighborhood, far and near, by land and by water, was kept in a state to which plague, pestilence, and starvation, are no more than 'a huckleberry to a persimmon' " (32).

Although Jonathan minds his own business during his neighbors' disputes, the Squire begins to kidnap Jonathan's rowers and keeps them for whole years in his boats, where they are forced to fight almost any boat they meet. When Jonathan consults his wife about this outrage, she, being "one of the most whimsical, cross-grained, contradictory and bedevilled termagants, that ever fell to the lot of mortal man," expresses "at least *seventeen* different opinions" (42).

When Jonathan finally writes the Squire in protest, Bull answers "that he did not in the least mean to hurt his good friend and loving son Jonathan; but was merely doing these things to spite his arch enemy Beau Napperty" (78–79). Jonathan tells him in reply "that he did not see the sense of threshing Beau Napperty over his shoulders, and what was more, he would not submit to it from any man, not even his own father" (79). Needing a new sword and pistols to back up his challenge and having little money because of his extravagant wife, Jonathan tries to borrow money from his tenants in lieu of raising their rents. They refuse to lend him any though, even the boatmen of Yankeyland [New England] for whose sake he was drawn into the quarrel. He finally makes do, however, and sends the Squire a "great challenge," but as the "history" concludes, we learn that Jonathan's overseers in Oniono [Connecticut], Martha's Vineyard [Massachusetts], and Rogues Island [Rhode Island] have "all set to work to prevent the honest man from having a fair chance of getting the better of Bull" (306).

Soon after Paulding's book appeared, its satire against the New England states provoked a heated book-length response, *The Beauties of Brother Bull-Us* (1812), which ridiculed Bull-us, praised the character and courage of New Englanders, and denounced Madison's administration. Quite possibly because he wished to promote national unity,[17] Paulding moderated his criticism of New England in subsequent editions. For the 1813 New York edition, he deleted his attacks on Oniono, Martha's Vineyard, and Rogues Island; inspired by the War of 1812, then in progress, he also intensified his satire of John Bull throughout and added five chapters elaborating upon Bull's provocation of Jonathan and describing how Bull's boats were bested by his son's (a reference to recent American naval victories).

For the 1835 edition of *Diverting History*, published as part of his collected works, Paulding added fifteen more chapters to the end of the book dealing with the various travelers Squire Bull had sent over to pry into Jonathan's private affairs. Eight British travel-writers receive separate and rather repetitious satirizing, but the only memorable treatment of the lot is that of Mrs. Trollope, primarily because it is the most pointedly nasty. Paulding introduces her as an ugly old trollope who "sold fish and muscles [*sic*] about the manor of Bullock; but owing to her carrying a d---l of a tongue in her head, and abusing everybody that tried to beat down her prices, had gradually got rather low in the world" (124). Squire Bull buys her some new clothes and sends her over the mill pond, where she visits one of Jonathan's new settlements and is treated kindly. She eventually falls into a roaring passion though, because the men "one and all resolutely declined making love to the old creature, who, now that she was dressed out so fine, had a notion that she was a beauty" (127). After denouncing them as a "tobacco-chewing, spitting, gouging, fast-eating, sling-drinking set," she slaps herself on her backside, "to show her breeding" (129), and makes tracks for the ancient manor of Bullock.

Although *Diverting History* is thoroughly anti-British, it owes a great deal in content and method to eighteenth-century British satires, particularly John Arbuthnot's *The History of John Bull* (1712) and Swift's *Gulliver's Travels* (1726).[18] Paulding called his book "a political allegory in the manner of Swift" (*Letters*, 170), yet ultimately it falls far short of Swift's achievements in this genre, because it lacks sufficient consistency and credibility on the literal level to endow it with lasting interest. Although Amos L. Herold has said that in *Diverting History* "Paulding came near striking off a little masterpiece of political satire,"[19] this estimate flatters. The work in all versions is dated, and if published today would engage few readers other than those with uncommon historical knowledge and interest. Furthermore, it has serious artistic flaws. First, the allegory periodically falters due to Paulding's attempt to provide correspondences for too many historical circumstances and events. We are told, for example, that Jonathan's wives are chosen by his tenants, which on the allegorical level makes sense, but on the literal level is absurd. Similarly, the treatment of political affairs is superficial and cursory due to his unwise decision to cover some 250 years' worth of "history" in less than 200 pages. Finally, the satire of the series of travel-writers at the end of the 1835 edition results in some fifty pages of anticlimax, for eventually his imagination failed him, and he made his sketches repetitious and boring.

What can be said for *Diverting History* is that it contains some entertaining allegorical truths. The relationships between Bull and Jonathan and their respective wives become amusingly convincing at times. Also, the national characters of England and the United States are occasionally brought to life in a humorous manner, with plausible explanations of international affairs offered in terms of their cartoonlike personalities. Later writers were to profit from Paulding's example in this regard, and, as Luther S. Mansfield has pointed out, *Diverting History* "set the tone and indeed to a large degree the pattern for a series of nationalistic political satires."[20] Among these, Irving's sketch "John Bull" (1819) and Melville's *Mardi* (1849) have achieved the most recognition.

John Bull in America

Paulding's last book-length contribution to the Paper War was his best. *John Bull in America, or, The New Munchausen* (1825) is a hilarious burlesque that has retained its freshness and humor over the course of time even though the objects of its satire have long been forgotten. The volume contains some excellent examples of native American humor, particularly the tall tale,[21] but its real strength lies in Paulding's creation of his first-person narrator, John Bull, and the consistently ironic treatment he accords him. Bull, obviously intended as a caricature of the British travel-writer, shows himself to be pompous, rude, credulous, prejudiced, and cowardly through his own self-serving account of his travels, and as Harold E. Hall has pointed out, in the process he "comes very near to life."[22]

Only occasionally does Paulding's characterization of the "author" of this volume strike a false note, as when Bull relates he has learned that in America pigs can vote; a grunt "was always considered," he says, "as a suffrage in favour of the democratic ticket, and a squeak for the federal or aristocratic party."[23] Most of the time, Bull's observations differ only in degree from those of actual British travelers. A comparison of the topics in his chapter titles with those in Janson's *The Stranger in America* (1807) makes this clear. Here are some of Janson's (in the order in which they appear):

Boston—Excessive Heat—Bed-bugs and Musquitoes—Manners of the Inhabitants—Effect of Republican Principles—Journey to Philadelphia—Miserable Roads—Communicative Passenger—Punishments Inflicted on Criminal Offenders—Washington, the Federal City and Seat of Government—Causes of the Deplorable State of the City—The Drama—Indecorous Behaviour of an American Audience—Deplorable Effects of the Uncontrolled Liberty Allowed to Youth in America—Smoking—An Academic Frolic—Gouging—Biting—Kicking—Treatment of Slaves—Barbarities Exercised on Them.[24]

Here are some of John Bull's (rearranged to parallel Janson's):

Arrives at Boston, the Capital of the State of Kennebuck—Gross and Impertinent Freedoms in Republicans—Quantity of Flies and Moschetoes—Law Against Killing Spiders—Manners of the People—Turbulent Spirit of Democracy—Intemperance—Ignorance—Impudence—Barbarity—Infamous Roads—Infamous Stage-Drivers—Privilege of Speech, Alias Impudent Loquacity—Sympathy in Favour of Rogues Here, and Reasons for It—Total Neglect of Education—House of Representatives Obliged to Have a Clerk to Read for Them—Theatre—Plays and Actors, all English—Miserable Effects of Freedom—Republican Lies—Republican Students—Republican Frolic—Astonishing Number of People with One Eye, or Two Black Eyes—Gouging—Turbulent Spirit of Democracy—Eating Negroes—Cruelty.

Paulding obviously exaggerates for satirical effect, but as the comparison shows, he does so less than an uninformed reader might believe.

The Preface to the narrative proper contains some wit as Paulding, posing as "editor," discusses the manuscript left in a hotel room by an Englishman who, traveling to New Orleans on business, has mysteriously disappeared. From what he has gathered, the "editor" says, its "author" was a "rather genteel looking stranger," about five feet ten with "a nose like a potato" (iii). Apparently, he also was "one of the principal writers of the Quarterly Review," because he writes with the "same classical severity and mildness of rebuke" (ix) and "seems never to have had the Quarterly out of mind (xi).

The "author" begins his narrative by declaring that previous to his departure, his impressions of America were favorable, adding, "I also fully believed that the people were a bundling, gouging, drinking, spitting, impious race, without either morals, literature, religion, or refinement" (2). On his trip over, he passes his time by reading the *Quarterly*, and he refers to this volume later, whenever he is in doubt about how to interpret his observations—that is, constantly.

His visit begins in Boston, and there he finds Negroes beaten for amusement, blood stains everywhere on the pavement, and a distinguished lady "occasionally amusing herself with turning round and scratching [her black servant's] face till it was covered with blood" (6). Next to this cruelty to Negroes, "the most common objects seen in the streets of Boston, are drunken men, women and children" (7). Fevers and agues afflict everyone, and "besides this, they have earthquakes and innundations, three times a week if not more" (9).

His first excursion is to Charleston, "the capital of the state of North Carolina, a city famous for eating negroes. It is about three miles from Boston" (13). He dines there with a Charleston judge and his family and reports: "There was a very suspicious dish on the table, which they called terrapin soup, in which I observed what had exactly the appearance of the fingers and toes of little negroes. I afterwards learned that this was actually the case and that terrapin is the cant name for black childern [*sic*], as papoose is for those of the Indians" (16).

He soon tires of Charleston, and "desirous of getting to New-Orleans as early as possible," he takes "a seat in the stage for Portsmouth, New Hampshire" (19). On the way, he meets a genial Frenchman who tries to give him directions, but only succeeds in irritating and frightening him. "If I know myself, I have no national prejudices," the "author" writes, "but I do hate Frenchmen" (21). When he stops at Portsmouth, "the capital of Georgia," he hears a disturbance at his inn: "On running in to see what was the matter, we found a son of the landlord, (who by the way was a general,) about eight years of age had thrown his mother down on the floor, and was beating, biting, scratching, and mauling her in a dreadful manner, while the general stood by laughing and clapping his hands in ecstasy. . . . Such are the first lessons of children in this chosen land of bundling, gouging, drunkenness, impertinence, impiety—and, to sum all up in one word, *democracy*" (37).

He next sets off for New Orleans once more on a road that "carried us through the states of Ohio, Alabama, and Connecticut" (39). He refuses to talk to anyone and becomes convinced that the Frenchmen and a "communicative traveller" plan to rob him because of their civilities. Nevertheless, he becomes an expert on American manners; "the white people," he says, "were for the most part employed in getting drunk at the taverns, running horses, fighting cocks, or gouging one another's eyes out—the women sitting along the road, chewing tobacco, and spitting in the faces of passers by; and the little boys and girls were pretty much engaged in beating their parents" (40).

Eventually in the course of his travels he visits other sites: New York City, where on the battery he sees "thousands of people, strutting, or rather staggering, about in dirty finery" (89); Philadelphia, where he learns that Jefferson is "at this moment, an actor on the Philadelphia boards for bread" (168); and Pine Woods, a frontier settlement, where he stays overnight with a backwoods family who almost frighten him to death. In this latter adventure, the best developed in the book, Paulding makes it clear that this large, poor, uneducated family treats the "author" with the utmost kindness, for they feed him a marvelous meal, insist that he sleep in their best bed, and try to make sure nothing disturbs his sleep. Meanwhile, he at first regards them with disgust; then, having seen their rifles, he assumes they are banditti, intent on murdering him in the night.

Staying awake out of fear, he reads the *Quarterly*, but this, he says, "only added to my boding apprehensions. As I read of the *gougings, bundlings, dirkings*, and *guessings*; of roasting alive on red-hot log fires—of ten dollars being the price of a man's life in this country, and of all the diabolical horrors of turbulent democracy, my spirit failed me, and I sunk insensibly on the floor" (203). He survives, of course, and as his narrative ends, he is in a hotel in Washington mulling over the *Quarterly.*

John Bull in America, written as Paulding's four-year-old son, William Irving, lay dying with a painful, lingering, unknown malady, is not only his most lighthearted and funny contribution to the Paper War, but also his most triumphant. The British periodicals unanimously praised it and laughingly admitted the validity of its satire. The *Literary Gazette* called it "a *genuine* and very clever *jeu d'esprit*," and liked best "the spirit and humour in which it is begun and ended." "There is no sourness or acrimony," the reviewer writes, and "the caricature we consider to be perfectly fair,—his prejudices not offensive, and we promise even the most national of our readers a hearty laugh at the droll exaggerations of John Bull's peculiarities."[25] The *News of Literature and Fashion* found it "a very agreeable extravagance" and declared, "our prejudiced and unfortunate countryman is a *caricature*, . . . *of course.* But there are many touches of great truth, unfortunately, and poignancy, in the drawing."[26] The *Lady's Magazine* and the *Monthly Magazine or British Register* also praised the book and its tone. Only *Blackwood's*, in a review written by the American John Neal posing as a British critic, offered grudging, rather than wholehearted, praise. Neal speculated that Paulding wrote it to get even with the *Quarterly* for its treatment of *A Sketch of Old England*, and he called it "a very clever, saucy, ill-tempered book; with a deal of snappish rough satire in it; much biting truth; and a sort of laboured cross-humour, at which you cannot help laughing, bitter and surly as it is."[27]

Perhaps out of perversity, or low spirits resulting from his son's death, Paulding disagreed with these favorable critical estimates. When Irving wrote him in the summer of 1825, mentioning his enjoyment of the book and its English reception, Paulding replied: "I am glad you were amused with the squib against the Quarterly. You know under what circumstances it was written, and I have only to add in excuse for its crudities, that it was actually begun and finished in three weeks' time. As a mere temporary thing, I did not in truth think it worth while to take any pains with its revisal; and circumstances occurred that tore my mind from all such matters. That it should be well received in England is what I never anticipated, and is one of the absolute eccentricities of John Bull, I think" (*Letters*, 83). Although one twentieth-century critic, Amos L. Herold, perhaps influenced by Paulding's own disparagement, has said that "to a modern reader the book seems to be wasted effort," another, Floyd C. Watkins, has come closer to the truth in calling it "probably Paulding's supreme extant achievement in humor."[28] Historically regarded, of course, the book represents more than mere entertainment; by triumphantly satirizing those British writers who wounded American pride throughout the Paper War, *John Bull in America* offered Americans, if only temporarily, the self-respect of requital, the satisfaction of revenge.

Chapter Four

Poetry

Throughout his adult life, Paulding regularly wrote poetry, though he approached this activity more as an eager apprentice than a meticulous craftsman. Believing that "a little occasional rugged carelessness is no blemish, when taken into view as part of a whole" (*Letters*, 60), he tended to write hastily when the spirit moved him and to spend little time correcting and polishing. He published two book-length poems, *The Lay of the Scottish Fiddle* (1813) and *The Backwoodsman* (1818), and at least forty-two shorter pieces that appeared in contemporary periodicals. In addition, he carefully transcribed fifty-three unpublished poems, along with twenty-one published ones, into a copy book now in the possession of the University of Pennsylvania Library.[1]

For the most part, Paulding's poetry uses forms, meters, imagery, and diction borrowed from the eighteenth-century writers he admired, such as Dryden, Pope, and Goldsmith, and it seldom contains any fresh or significant insights that allow it to approach its models in excellence. Occasionally, however, one or more of Paulding's three main strengths as a writer—an excellent sense of humor, the ability to tell a good story, and a willingness to experiment with original subjects and themes—raises his poetry, particularly his two long narrative poems, above the commonplace. In fact, parts of *The Backwoodsman* show him handling American subjects and themes with considerable skill and originality, and the book as a whole represents a notable overlooked contribution to American literature.

The Lay of the Scottish Fiddle

Paulding's first volume of verse, *The Lay of the Scottish Fiddle; A Tale of Havre de Grace, supposed to be written by Walter Scott, Esq.* (1813), is a parody of Scott's *Lay of the Last Minstrel* (1805), which Paulding's readers knew well. Scott, who captivated American audiences with his Waverley novels during the second and third decades of the century, initially thrilled and delighted Americans with his poetry. His first three metrical romances, *The Lay of the Last Minstrel, Marmion* (1808), and *The Lady of the Lake* (1810), based on old Scottish Border legends, became the most avidly and widely read books in the United States during the first decades of the century. As James D. Hart has pointed out, the American romantic temper of the times "wanted heroic action, rich color, and exciting pageantry," and "these it found simply and melodiously set forth in Scott's poems. . . ."[2] Recalling "the general intoxication" with Scott, the publisher Samuel Goodrich wrote: "these productions seized powerfully upon the popular mind. Everybody could read and comprehend them. One of my younger sisters committed the whole of the Lady of the Lake to memory, and was accustomed of an evening to sit at her sewing, while she recited it to an admiring circle of listeners. All young poets were inoculated with the octa-syllabic verse, and newspapers, magazines, and even volumes, teemed with imitations and variations inspired by the 'Wizard Harp of the North.' "[3]

To Paulding, whose family had experienced the sufferings and hardships of actual border warfare, Scott's romantic recreations were offensive, and his antipathy to Scott, which was lifelong, acquired aesthetic and political dimensions as it developed; like Twain, he condemned Scott's works as pernicious because they distorted reality and inculcated in their readers an admiration for obsolete social ideals and false standards of behavior. Many know that Twain in *Life on the Mississippi* (1883) blamed Scott for the American Civil War and accused him of setting "the world in love with dreams and phantoms . . . with the sillinesses and emptiness, sham grandeurs, sham gauds, and sham chivalries of a brainless and worthless long-vanished society."[4] What few realize, however, is that Paulding had indicted Scott on similar grounds seventy years earlier in *The Lay of the Scottish Fiddle.*[5]

Paulding was convinced that the barbaric conduct of the British naval officers during the War of 1812 (in progress as he wrote his poem) "arose in a great measure from a vehement desire to imitate the pernicious examples, held up in those mischievous books of chivalry, from time to time manufactured by [Scott]."[6] In his *Lay*, Paulding both ridicules Scott's poetry and castigates the conduct of the British by portraying the British naval commanders as modern border chieftains and their military actions in the Chesapeake as pillage and plunder, which, in fact, they were.

In early April of 1813, some four months before the publication of Paulding's poem,[7] the British fleet, under Admiral Sir John Bolase Warren, moved up the Chesapeake, looting and burning the towns along its banks. Warren, an enervated sixty-year-old veteran of the Napoleonic Wars, let his second in command, Rear Admiral Sir George Cockburn, an aggressive forty-year-old combat officer, carry out the British campaign of terror and attrition. After threatening the city of Baltimore, and plundering various islands, Cockburn attacked Frenchtown on April 29 at the head of the Elk River and burned its wharf, fishery, and warehouses. Four days later, he led a surprise attack at dawn on Havre de Grace, meeting little resistance. The local militia fled after a few shots, with the exception of John O'Neill, an Irishman who remained to man the guns. O'Neill was injured, captured, and imprisoned, and after the town was plundered, forty of its sixty buildings were burned by the invaders. Subsequently, on May 5 Cockburn's squadron attacked and burned Georgetown and Fredericktown, and on June 25 seized the town of Hampton, where some of the British troops—the Chasseurs Britannique (French prisoners enlisted in British service)—committed various atrocities.[8] According to one eye-witness, Sir Charles James Napier, a British officer, "Every horror was perpetrated with impunity—rape, murder, pillage—*and not a man was punished*."[9] By the summer of 1813, Warren and Cockburn had inspired the hatred of most Americans, including Paulding, and in his poem Paulding tried to convert his hatred into good-natured satire, with mixed success.

The *Lay* consists of a Preface, an Introduction, five cantos, and some one-hundred pages of nonsensical notes intended to mock Scott's prolix antiquarian scholarship. In the Introduction, Paulding ridicules Scott's portrayal of an infirm old harp-playing minstrel accompanied by an orphan boy, by presenting instead a blind old fiddler, led around by a little black dog. Having matched Scott's pathos with bathos, Paulding then has the fiddler and his dog wander from New York to Princeton, where at "Lord" Joline's tavern, the fiddler begins to sing his lay.

In Canto I, entitled "The Three Knights," the scene is the quarter-deck of a British man-of-war, where Sir Bolus [Admiral Warren] summons Childe Cockburn [Rear Admiral Cockburn] and Sir Bereford [Captain John Bereford, whose four ships bombarded the town of Lewes with some 1,000 rounds in twenty-two hours on April 6, 1813][10] to help him decide "when and how / He might chastise the sinful fry, / Who dar'd HIS MAJESTY defy" (20). Paulding describes Beresford as a drunkard and a coward and Sir Cockburn as "a border chief," descended from thieves.

Having learned to steal as a child and having "early show'd how great he'd be / In feats of modern chivalry" (23), Cockburn eventually went to sea,

> For he had heard the valiant feats
> Of British tars and British fleets;
> That bullies of the subject seas,
> Not only rob their enemies,
> But claim the right, as Yankies know,
> To plunder friend as well as foe.
>
> (25)

Paulding's allusion, of course, is to the confiscation by British frigates of neutral American shipments bound for France, which precipitated the War of 1812.

In Canto II, "The Council," the three officers pore over the chart of Chesapeake Bay and gleefully resolve to burn Frenchtown and Havre de Grace. After Cockburn sings about feasting on "the fright, of the scampering wight, / And the terror of half-naked wench" (42), the three dance hand-in-hand the Irish jig and the Scottish reel, then dine, drink themselves into a stupor, and stagger off to bed.

In Canto III, "The Progress," the British sail up the Chesapeake looking for the "French" towns. As they approach Annapolis, the state leaders flee at the sight of Cockburn's fleet while the "sons of Tammany" turn out with bows and arrows to shoot errantly at a neighboring church. The Irish, on the other hand, are ready to battle, but when the fleet does not land, they settle for a bloody fist fight among themselves. Thus Paulding pokes well-deserved fun at the military prowess of his countrymen, who time and again made fools of themselves as they ineptly tried to defend the Chesapeake Bay region.[11]

Eventually the British spy the little rural town of Havre de Grace, but before Paulding describes its destruction, he uses the conclusion of Canto III and all of Canto IV, "The Digression," to insert an interlude of lusty roistering at "Lord" Joline's tavern. As the fiddler sleeps, the Princeton students drink and dance with Jersey maids and call for entertainment from Joline, who obliges with a song satirizing the college life:

> Professors! they preach and palaver, my boys,
> And prate of stiff *larning*, and cramp all your joys;
> They're paid for it too, then why should they not?
> It helps them to tipple and toss off the pot.
> Then whoop *Suthron lads!* sweet Margery—caress her!
> Drink deep—laugh and sing, and d--n the professor.
>
> (66)

A short time later, Joline dances with a flirtatious country girl with whom a young bumpkin is in love, and when the tavern keeper kisses her cheek, the boy strikes him in a jealous rage. As Joline falls to the floor, apparently dead, the collegians flee the tavern and events then parallel closely the opening of Scott's *Lay*, where Lady Buccleuch, widow of the recently slain Sir Walter Scott of Branksome, retires to her secret bower and uses witchcraft to plot revenge. Paulding's widow Joline, in her "book of witching grammary," discovers that the boy is in debt to the tavern and consequently has him imprisoned in the county jail.

After this lively but silly digression, the fiddler continues his lay with Canto V, "The Burning," where Paulding's humor turns to righteous indignation as he describes the destruction of Havre de Grace. He begins by relating how the local militia, after a few volleys,

> Agreed to quit the bloody fray;
> So donn'd their arms and ran away,
> To tell, with self-approving glee,
> Their wondrous feats of chivalry.
>
> (103)

"Valiant O'Neale" [John O'Neill], however, makes a futile attempt to "strike a spark of patriot ire" (109) in his fellow townspeople, until "Cockburn's men, as legends say, / Kidnapp'd, and carried him away" (112). The burning of the defenseless town, the suffering of women, infants, the bed-ridden, and the aged are melodramatically described, and the lay then comes to a forceful close with a "houseless matron" ironically praising the "Briton bold,"

> 'Who comes in pious christian ire
> 'To purify the earth by fire;
> 'Who labours for the world's repose
> 'By heaping up a world of woes;
> 'Who points our hopes to realms of bliss,
> 'By making us heart-sick of this;
> 'And thus, as farmer Caleb saith,
> 'ACTS AS THE "BULWARK OF OUR FAITH."'
>
> (120)

Although Paulding's "Notes," which follow, contain mostly lighthearted nonsense, such as lengthy discussions of such "ancient" ballads as "Heye Dyddle Dyddle" and "Owlde Kynge Cole," he occasionally satirizes what for him were serious subjects, such as Federalist Congressman Josiah Quincy's outspoken opposition to America's war effort, the airs of moral and intellectual superiority displayed by New Englanders, the false accounts of America promulgated by foreign travelers, and Scott's harmful influence on Cockburn, "whose youthful propensities were strengthened and matured by the alluring examples of William of Deloraine, Lord Marmion, . . . and other distinguished moss-troopers and Buccaneers" (220). At one point in the notes, Paulding, posing as Scott's editor, speculates that "Mr. S---- has turned Democrat" (219), and he thus resolves the paradox of a poem supposedly written by the Tory Scott that savagely attacks the British.

In both America and England, Paulding's *Lay* evoked praise mingled with reproach. In the *Analectic Magazine* his friend Irving applauded the "little passages of pathos and feeling" and "the descriptions of American scenery, and American manners," which were "touched off with much truth of pencil and felicity of manner." As a Federalist and anglophile, however, Irving felt obliged to lament that "the revising hand of the author had not expunged" the "traces of political satire . . . as they are calculated to awaken angry feelings in some bosoms, and to injure the interests of a work, which would otherwise be read with pleasure and approbation throughout the union."[12] (Irving's review appeared in September 1813; on August

24, 1814, the British invaded the city of Washington and burned the Capitol, the White House, the Treasury, War and Navy offices, the depository of the national library and public records. Outraged, Irving enlisted in the New York militia.)[13]

When the *Lay* was republished in London in 1814, the English editor introduced the poem with ambivalent comments similar to Irving's. While praising Paulding's talent, he finds it "a pity that the author should have descended to burlesque and parody," and he predicts that Paulding will attain "immortal honour" by "disdaining to catch at a laugh; and by determining not to give up to party, or even to vindictive patriotism, a soul meant for mankind."[14]

From the British *Quarterly Review*, Paulding's poem received no such half-hearted praise, but instead, pure venom. As mentioned in chapter 3, the reviewer used the work as an excuse to castigate the American people, but he finally turned to the poem and declared, "The story we can scarcely discover; the tendency is sufficiently clear—to calumniate the naval officers of Old England, and to libel its own countrymen of New England." Calling the author "very angry and very scurrilous," the reviewer argues that the burning of Havre de Grace was caused by "Mr. Madison's invasion of Canada" and that "a spark from the fire which the Americans lighted on the shores of Ontario, spread the conflagration to the banks of the Chesapeake." After further denigrating Paulding's criticism of the Federalists, the reviewer concludes by declaring: "We have waded through the text with weariness, and through the notes with contempt for the author's powers, and indignation at his principles: he is the libeller of every thing in America that is not mean and wicked."[15]

Although the political satire of Paulding's poems thus elicited contemporary disapproval, it is the main source of the interest the poem still retains. Little can be said for the literary value of the work, for its use of rhythm and rhyme is careless, its structure slovenly, and its treatment of characters and events superficial; nevertheless, it contains amusing satirical passages and sheds revealing historical light upon both the vogue of Scott and the War of 1812.

The Backwoodsman

During the five years following the publication of the *Lay*, Paulding thought about material for his second long poem in which he wished to deal seriously with the unique features of his own country. Although his political views had dominated his first four books, in his fifth, *The Backwoodsman,* he subordinated these views to his primary concern, the introduction of American character types, American settings, and American history. Obviously guided in his efforts by the need for a national literature, Paulding in his Preface declares that the author's object is "to indicate to the youthful writers of his native country, the rich poetic resources with which it abounds." Ironically, in America the poem was ridiculed for its unusual subject matter, American settlers and Indians on the Ohio frontier, in Britain praised, with the *Edinburgh Literary Journal* citing its author as one of "the four poets of greatest eminence which America at present possesses."[16] Paulding, at several periods in his life, worked at revising and rewriting his experimental poem, but he never completed the task. Even in its original version, however, the poem, now rare and forgotten, deserves recognition for its innovative features, particularly its use of the Indian.

Overall *The Backwoodsman* contains about 3,200 lines in heroic couplets and is divided into six books. The first three focus on a tenant farmer named Basil who, after struggling with poverty and sickness in the Hudson River Valley, yearns for the "glowing West."[17] Although Basil's neighbors tell him stories of wolves, bears, and "bloody Indians," the thought of freedom inspires him, so after saying goodbye to friends and praying at the grave of his parents, he sets off with his family.

Their departure provides Paulding the opportunity to describe the beauty of the Hudson River Valley landscape as Basil looks back upon it from near Fort Putnam. The scene, which includes West Point below, the Hudson Highlands beyond to the north, and the Catskills in the far distance, later became a favorite of the Hudson River School of painters, a number of whom, including Asher Durand, John G. Chapman, and Robert W. Weir, sought Paulding out as a patron or friend and drew inspiration from his pioneering use of the American landscape in his works.[18] Two paintings that capture on canvas Paulding's description of Basil's parting view are Robert Havell, Jr.'s, *West Point from Fort Putnam* (ca. 1850) and John Ferguson Weir's *View of the Highlands from West Point* (1862).[19]

Basil's travels through New Jersey and Pennsylvania in Books

I and II comprise the weakest part of the poem, for here the narrative has little forward thrust and no suspense, except that generated by a thunderstorm the family encounters on the western side of the Alleghenies. In Book III, however, the narrative gains pace and interest as Paulding has Basil and his family join a little band of pioneers in Pittsburgh and travel down the Ohio until they reach their new home in the wilderness, where they build "a little rustic village." At the end of Book III, however, the narrative flags briefly again, for after relating that Basil prospers, Paulding becomes uncertain about what else to say about him.

In Book IV, he resolves this dilemma by shifting his focus to an isolated Indian, once the proud chief of a thousand red-men, but now "The last of all his race" (89). Throughout the last three books, then, Basil is forgotten as Paulding becomes more and more absorbed in presenting the struggle, both physical and ideological, between Indians and whites.

His main Indian character, whom he calls the Prophet, is based on the half-blind Shawnee medicine man, Tenskwatawa, known as the Prophet, who was the twin brother of Tecumseh and joined with him in inspiring a religious revival among the tribes of the Northwest and uniting them into an Indian confederacy in the years prior to the War of 1812. In Books IV and V, the Prophet's unsuccessful quest for revenge develops into the strongest, most taut and dramatic part of the poem. While Paulding had little sympathy for the Indian character or vision, he understood well righteous indignation, outrage, and defiance, and thus he was able to present the Prophet more realistically and convincingly than any of his other characters.

Obviously a type of the Byronic hero, Paulding's Prophet most closely resembles a later avatar of Byronism, Melville's Ahab, and Paulding's attitude toward him—one of both attraction and repulsion—matches Melville's toward his ungodly, godlike captain. Like Ahab, the Prophet is a monomaniac, bent upon revenge, whose suffering and grief endow him with a degree of tragic greatness. Although able to inflame others and engage them in the quest, he eventually destroys both them and himself, but not before first defying his god for seeming to betray him and then stabbing his hated white enemy at the moment of his death.

Paulding introduces the Prophet at the beginning of Book IV by explaining how "brooding o'er one bloody theme," his "brain to moody madness was beguil'd" (91). The Indian roams alone at night, sometimes climbing to the tops of cliffs in midnight storms, deliriously communing with the thunder and lightning. As a result, he comes to believe "He had commission from his God receiv'd, / The remnant of his fallen race to save" (93). Although obviously raving mad, the Prophet, when he preaches to his fellow Indians, displays an eloquence and perceptivity that impress. He tells the tribes that when the whitemen first came to America, the countless Indians extended help and goodwill, while the whites responded "with fraud and lies," making the Indians renounce "their ancient gods throughout the land / For other creeds they could not understand." "Thus," the Prophet continues,

> ". . . debas'd by Christian arts,
> "Weaken'd their bodies, and corrupt their hearts,
> "Tribe after tribe, soon found a timeless grave,
> "Or liv'd to be the white-man's abject slave,
> "Linger'd amid the scorn of every fool,
> "And lick'd the dust, where they were born to rule."
>
> (96)

As the Prophet's speech concludes, it becomes more extreme, yet always logical; after exhorting the warriors not to spare any of the whites, even babies, he adds, "Vainly we kill the root, if still the seed, / Within the soil is left, more foes to breed" (98).

At the end of the Prophet's speech, another Indian character, a wise youth who rules despotically over distant tribes, comes to the fore. This "young Shawanoe" (100), obviously modeled on Tecumseh, is inspired by the truth of "the wandering maniac's mission" (100), and prepares to put into action "one great plan to free his wand'ring race, / Or give them death, and rid them of disgrace" (99). The next morning the Indians pray to their "Great Spirit," asking him for his guidance and aid, and Book IV ends with the Indians convinced that the Spirit "loves our tribe, he sees, he feels our woes. / And gives us vengeance, on our ruthless foes" (105).

Book V contains the most original and compelling portion of the poem, for it is here that Paulding dramatizes, by means of an engaging dialogue between the Prophet and a mysterious spokesman for American Christian civilization, the ideological struggle between Indians and whites. At the beginning of the episode, the Prophet takes an excursion alone to a hill overlooking the white man's village, there recalling his childhood spent on the same spot, and after turning away with sadness and resentment, he sees a saintly aged Pilgrim who "seem'd like patriarch of some distant age, / Return'd awhile to linger on this stage" (122). When asked why he is in the forest, the Pilgrim replies that he plans to preach to the Indian about the Bible and the true God, to which the Prophet replies, "you have no other god than Gold" (123), and after citing how the whites have been corrupted by money, urges, "ere for distant converts thus you roam, / See if there's nothing left to do at home" (124).

Unabashed, the Pilgrim tells the Indian that Christian whites "Shall lead thee to bright paths of peace and joy, / The arts of life, and social comforts teach, / And happiness beyond thy fancy's reach" (124), but the Prophet rejects this offer by asserting, with more than a little accuracy,

> "I know what things your Christian Indians are!
> "O! I have seen them naked and forlorn,
> "Of every attribute of manhood shorn,
> "Skulking from town to town, a worthless race,
> "Earning the wages of their deep disgrace."
>
> (125)

The Prophet then asks whether the uncorrupted Indian warriors who can track better than whites, tell time by the sun and stars, and endure torture in silence are not men. The Pilgrim's reply is that they are men who disgrace their Maker, whose gods are imps from hell, and whose mercy is torture; "Alas!" he says, "the ruthless thing that never spares, / Is not a man, though manhood's form he wears" (126).

The Prophet's response to the charge of being unmerciful represents one of the most penetrating passages in the poem, for with telling truth he declares:

> "And dost *thou* prate of mercy! O, full well,
> "Of Christian mercies can our Indians tell!
> "You spar'd their lives, to drive them from their home,
> "Like scouting beasts in distant wilds to roam;
> "You did not kill them, like a generous foe,

"And end their sufferings with one manly blow;
"You spar'd them for long exile, and disgrace,
"Spar'd them to see the ruin of their race,
"Spar'd them for keener tortures, woes more dire
"Than scalping-knife, or slow consuming fire."
(127)

He then asks the Pilgrim if he would praise the mercy of a foe who reft him of home, family, and race and left him "Loathing the present as a bitter curse, / Fearing the future, that still threaten'd worse" (129).

Echoing Pope's "Essay on Man," the Pilgrim answers with what strikes the modern reader as unsatisfying Christian fatalism. He tells the Prophet,

"... learn of me, Thou lone and wretched man,
" 'Tis impious the ways of GOD to scan.
"For so it is, alas! or right or wrong,
"The weak are ever victims of the strong.
(130)

He then offers an empty promise by declaring that if the Indians forgive and forget, the white man will bless their weakness and "Give them rich lands, where they may dwell in peace, / And every passing year their stores increase" (132). Only the poem's date of composition excuses Paulding's lack of irony here. (The removal of the Eastern Indian tribes from their reservations, one of the most disgraceful actions in our national history, would begin some ten years later.)

The Prophet's final response contains appropriate disgust and anger, as he reminds the Pilgrim that his tribesmen are dead and then cries, "Were I a Christian I would scalp thee now; / Go home, and lye amid thy very pray'rs, / And say the bloody Indian never spares" (132). The Pilgrim then sighs, turns away, and, according to Paulding, marvels "That men were born with such a stubborn mind, / And hearts so hard, and eyes so wilful blind" (133). Although here and throughout the dialogue, the Pilgrim clearly speaks for the author, the Prophet, benefiting from Paulding's ability to empathize, transcends the weaker role intended for him and through the dignity of his character and the truth of his words enlists the sympathies of the reader in his cause.

Book VI of the poem is anticlimactic, although its subject is bloody battle between Indians and whites, modeled roughly on the Battle of Tippecanoe. A night scene on the banks of a woodland stream where a thousand fires gleam red on either side precedes the battle, and at dawn it begins, with Paulding declining to describe it in detail, asking, "Why . . . should I luxuriate in gore, / And tell of horrors often told before?" (159). Instead, he generally relates the carnage that follows and tells how when the Prophet fell, the Indians gave up and slowly left the field "with dangling arms, and melancholly grace—" (162), while the whites "hung upon their rear, / And mow'd them like the ripen'd harvest ear" (162). The simile, quite appropriate for these farmer-soldiers, is so callous as to seem intentionally ironic; however, it is most likely not, given its context.

A death scene climaxes Book VI, as Paulding returns his focus to the Prophet, whose life blood slowly drains drop by drop. As he dies, he anticipates Ahab in "The Candles" chapter of *Moby-Dick*, by thus addressing his god:

> "Great Spirit! ev'n in this my dying hour,
> "I do defy thee, fearless of thy power,
> "Be it thy want of might, or lack of will,
> "Or one or both, I do defy thee still. . . .
> "If thou hadst power, why then refuse thine aid,
> "If not, then have thy vot'ries idly pray'd;
> "Thou art a cheat that in the heav'ns dost dwell,
> "Take my defiance, and so fare thee well."
>
> (168–69)

At the moment of death, the Prophet stabs a wounded white man lying beside him, but the man he thus kills is his ally, a European renegade.

Paulding concludes his poem by telling the reader that peace, happiness, and freedom reigned after the whites' victory and that his tale is done; as an afterthought, however, he adds that Old Basil has grown gray and "waxes in wealth and honours every day" (173). An eminent judge, general, congressman, he is loved by all and as happy as can be. Thus, with this awkward pivot toward the poem's initial direction, Paulding brings it to an end.

Soon after its appearance, *The Backwoodsman* received rough treatment at the hands of Paulding's American contemporaries, who scorned the literary trail he had blazed. In a sixteen-page review that appeared in the *American Monthly and Critical Review*, the reviewer, "G.," claims that "the state of society in America . . . does not, at present, furnish materials either sufficiently abundant or various for the higher species of poetry." Poetry should treat "the marvellous and magnificent," "the pathetic and the beautiful," "the superlative and aristocratic," he asserts; thus Basil's rustic character is "about as little adapted to shine in a poetical garb or capacity as can well be imagined."[20] Although "G." quotes a number of passages from the poem and praises them, he finds Paulding's American materials too vulgar for his taste and concludes by arguing against the desire to produce a national poetry.

Two prominent New York writers also focused on the poem's subject matter and ridiculed it, causing Paulding to declare in a January 1820 letter to Irving: "My unfortunate poem has been over and over again attacked by the combined powers of wit and dullness, the former led by a wicked wag called *Croaker*, the latter by our old friend H. . . . Had I not been built of stubborn oak, seasoned in the school of poverty, like an old chimney-piece in a log house, I should sometimes have scratched my head a little to find if I had any brains" (*Letters*, 60). The Croaker was Joseph Rodman Drake, whose satiric verses in the *New York Evening Post* for March 18, 1819, ridiculed Paulding as "the pride of the Backwood! / The poet of cabbages, log huts, and gin."[21] The "H." Paulding refers to was Fitz-Greene Halleck, a friend of Drake's, whose popular satire of New York society, *Fanny* (1819), declared, "Homer was well enough; but would he ever / Have written, think ye, the Backwoodsman? never." Although Halleck cites Paulding as a superb writer of satire, he adds, "Why is he sipping weak Castalian dews? / The muse has damned him—let him damn the muse."[22] (Some fifty years later and after Paulding's death, Halleck expressed a more favorable estimate of Paulding and his poem, writing Evert Duyckinck that Paulding "had great honor as a writer, and great merit as a man. He thought clearly and bravely, and spoke as he thought. His two lines alluding to our revolutionary soldiers, wherein he says they 'Saved this good land and when the tug was o'er, / Begged their way home at every scoundrel's door,' are a specimen of his manner of expression when indignantly battling for the right against the wrong."[23])

Ironically, in Britain Paulding's poem received much kinder treatment where its Americanness was considered a virtue not a fault. In August 1819 the *British Review* declared that "the most recent, as well as the best specimen of American poesy is unquestionably the 'Backwoodsman of Mr. Paulsen [*sic*]. . . . His versification is uniformly smooth, and animated with glowing sentiments of liberty, according to the *American* model." The *New Monthly Magazine*, in February 1820, called the poem "One of the most favourable specimens of native poetical ability that we have yet been presented with by transatlantic genius." Similarly, in November 1820 the *Monthly Review Enlarged* observed that " 'The Backwoodsman' possesses considerable merit, and is curious from the subject and the manners which it portrays."[24] Several years later, when selections from the poem appeared along with others by Halleck, Bryant, and a group of lesser writers in *Specimens of the American Poets* (London, 1822), Paulding gained additional favorable attention from a number of British reviewers, and by 1829 his reputation as a poet was so well established in Britain that the authoritative *Edinburgh Literary Journal*, as previously mentioned, cited him as one of America's four most eminent poets (the others being Bryant, Halleck, and Percival).

Paulding never brought out a new edition of *The Backwoodsman*, and over the years the 1818 volume has become rare and forgotten; only a few twentieth-century critics have mentioned it in passing, and they have dismissed it as rambling and dull. Rather curiously, one critic, Luther S. Mansfield, in the influential *Literary History of the United States*, states that the poem has "some sixteen hundred lines," when it actually has twice that many, and he describes it as the story of Basil's westward trek and successful western career, failing to mention that the second half of the poem focuses on the plight of the American Indian.[25]

Despite its neglect, *The Backwoodsman* has much to recommend it, particularly its innovative and complex portrayal of the Indian. Since the end of the eighteenth century, a number of American poems had dealt with the Indian, picturing him either as nature's nobleman or as a subhuman beast. Freneau, of course, celebrated the Indian's nobility in several shorter poems, published in his *Miscellaneous*

Works (1788), but the first long narrative poem to use the Indian as a central figure was Sarah Wentworth Morton's *Ouâbi* (1790), which also emphasized his nobility. Some thirty years later, as Roy Harvey Pearce has pointed out in his seminal study of the Indian, there emerged a series of narrative poems of a different type which attempted to make the destruction of the Indian "intelligible in relation to the progress of American civilization." "The pattern of these poems," Pearce explains, "is uniform enough itself to constitute a received way of imaging American relations with the Indians. The Indian is described for what he is, a noble savage. The coming of the white men is described for what it is, the introduction of agrarian civilization. And the Indian is shown dying or moving west, often with a vision of the great civilized life which is to come after him. . . . The tone is now bitter, now melancholy. The end is said to be good."[26]

Although *The Backwoodsman* is clearly related to this series and, in fact, seems to have been its forerunner, Pearce fails to mention the work, placing instead later poems such as Charles Mead's *Mississippian Scenery* (1819) and James Eastburn and Robert Sands' *Yamoyden* (1820) at the beginning of his list of titles in the series. Similarly, G. Harrison Orians, in his several studies of the treatment of the Indian in American literature, ignores *The Backwoodsman* and declares that "with *Yamoyden* (1820), by J. W. Eastburn and R. C. Sands, and *Sanillac* [1831], by Henry Whiting, the new type of metrical novel was well on its popular course; and in the years to follow many tales of Indian chieftains . . . were to run from the presses."[27] While *The Backwoodsman*'s pioneering treatment of the Indian's confrontation with civilization on the frontier has been overlooked in these and other modern historical and literary studies of the subject, the author invariably discussed in such studies, Cooper, knew and admired Paulding's poem to such a degree that he quoted four lines from it on the title page of *The Pioneers* (1823), the first book in his series of Leatherstocking Tales.

Paulding's originality certainly makes *The Backwoodsman* worthy of more attention than it has received; however, it is his vigorous and thoughtful treatment of his main Indian character that gives the poem its strength, engaging the reader's interest in a far more complex manner than other related, better-known metrical works such as

Longfellow's *Hiawatha* (1855), which idealizes and sentimentalizes the Indian, or the anonymous *Ensenore* (1840), which, drawing upon the tradition of the sensationalistic captivity narrative, portrays him as a treacherous, cruel barbarian, worthy of extinction. Regretably, the tension between sympathy and antipathy found in the poem does not characterize Paulding's earlier and later treatments of the Indian.

The Backwoodsman seems to have been written at a unique stage in the development of his thought on the subject; most typically, he portrayed the Indian as an ignoble savage, a viewpoint probably influenced by his 1815 encounter with Henry Bird, a stoic and diffident Ohio settler who had recently been released from Indian captivity. From Bird, Paulding acquired deep misgivings about Indian behavior as well as material he would use in *The Backwoodsman* and in his novel *Konigsmarke* (1823). In "The Adventures of Henry Bird," a journalistic piece based on an interview, Paulding presents a straightforward account of the torture Bird endured at the hands of the Shawnee. At one point during his captivity, Bird was tied to a stake and burned with fire brands on the hand and arm at half-hour intervals for an entire day. Paulding reports: "I saw him. . . . He had more than forty wounds—his shoulder was partly cut off, his thigh gashed with seams, his side scarred with a tomahawk, his fingers almost burnt off, and one of his arms in some places nearly bare to the bone."[28] One of Bird's captors was "the famous Shawanese Prophet, brother to Tecumseh," who, according to Bird, was "about fifty, very ill looking, and no warrior" (32). The Prophet was "considered to speak the will of the Great Spirit," and was "continually exhorting the Indians to fight the Americans, and keep them from taking away their lands" (32–33).

While Paulding's interview with Bird may explain the antipathy accorded the character of the Prophet in *The Backwoodsman*, to account for the sympathy shown him, one should probably consider the influence of Paulding's two friends Brevoort and Irving. In the summer of 1811, Brevoort had traveled to Mackinac, was distressed by the plight of the Indian tribes in the region, and had written Irving, enclosing, and requesting that he publish in a newspaper, "two genuine Indian Orations literally interpreted," one of which he had heard "spoken amidst an assemblage of 20 Chiefs with the most forcible & graceful elocution." He later added, "I wish Paulding & you or yrself [*sic*] alone to take the trouble of writing a prefatory note to the speeches."[29]

Although we do not know the results of this correspondence, we do know that within Irving, at least, Brevoort's concern and his firsthand material struck a responsive chord. His two essays, "Traits of Indian Character" and "Philip of Pokanoket," published in the February and June, 1814, issues of the *Analectic Magazine* and later republished in *The Sketch Book*, are clearly celebrations of the Indian's nobility. In the first, he argues that "there is something in the character and habits of the North American savage . . . that is, to my mind, wonderfully striking and sublime";[30] in the second, he praises King Philip's tribe as "a band of native untaught heroes; who made the most generous struggle of which human nature is capable; fighting to the last gasp in the cause of their country, without a hope of victory or a thought of renown. Worthy of an age of poetry, . . . they have left scarcely any authentic traces on the page of history, but stalk, like gigantic shadows in the dim twilight of tradition."[31]

Given his close friendships with Brevoort and Irving, and especially his respect for the latter, Paulding could not have been insensible to their attitude or free from its influence. In fact, when he informed Irving in a letter that *The Backwoodsman* had enabled him to portray Indian characters and manners, he knew that his friend would approve, given that his own sentiments had found expression there. Unfortunately, in Paulding's later fiction, he periodically evidenced an unalloyed form of literary racism, presenting Indians as "the most wild, the most revengeful, and the most impracticable of the human race."[32]

The Shorter Poems

Although *The Lay* and *The Backwoodsman* were Paulding's major poetic efforts, he also wrote approximately one hundred shorter poems throughout his life, with about half of these appearing in periodicals such as the *Analectic*, the *New-York Mirror*, and *Graham's*. Most are feeble and trite, and unfortunately the same can be said of most of the unpublished poems he transcribed in his copy book. Whereas his longer poems benefit from his narrative talent, his shorter poems suffer from its absence; nevertheless, he occasionally produced some respectable verse in this genre.

In his copybook, Paulding entered the dates of composition for many of his poems, and these, along with dates of publication, indicate that his poetic career can be roughly divided into three active periods, 1798–1804, 1812–1820, and 1840–1848, with one third of his efforts spread out over the remaining forty years of his adult life.

The poems of the first period, written when he was in his early twenties, deal with young love in the courtly tradition. He lavishes praise on his beloved, pays tribute to her physical beauty, and laments her treatment of him. Several poems also describe Hudson River Valley scenery, and a few are feeble attempts at political satire. The main weaknesses of these poems are their stock phrases and stale imagery. His descriptive lyrics, for example, are filled with "shadowy clouds of fleece," "bubbling brooks," "ever busy bees," and "balmy Spring," while his love poems focus on "love-begetting eyes," "rosebud lips," "throbbing bosoms," "snow white skin," and an assortment of birds, flowers, zephyrs, and stars.

During his second period of activity, when he was in his late thirties and early forties, most of Paulding's poems dealt with patriotic themes inspired by the War of 1812. Their titles indicate the range of topics covered: "The Volunteer," "The Stripes and Stars," "Ode on the National Apathy," "The Battle of Erie," "A Sailor's Elegy on the Fate of the Wasp." Five of the poems of this period are satirical and moral epigrams, and one entitled "The White and the Red Man" is a thoughtless meditation on the circumstances of the two races, concluding that the Indian's life is the more natural and carefree.

The best poem of this period, entitled "A Dreaming Oddity: Myself and the Doctor," contains 215 lines of blank verse describing a dream Paulding experienced. Published in the *American Monthly Magazine and Critical Review* (June 1818), the poem is remarkably free of trite diction and didactic statement. Some of the most interesting lines, echoing perhaps Shelley's *Alastor* (1816), tell of the author's journey with a beautiful, thinly clad lady, who appears riding on sea waves; as they ride together, the imagery becomes quite erotic, but Paulding was probably not conscious of this. In his notes to the poem, he tries to explain his dream by citing the conversation and meal he enjoyed before retiring, but it is the irrational, suggestive, and visionary quality of the poem that makes it engaging. Unfortunately, this quality appears in none of his other poetry.

During his third period of poetic activity, when he was in his sixties, Paulding dealt with a variety of topics, but courtly love and erotic dreams were not among them. Three of his poems are light verse satirizing poetasters and teetotalers; two, inspired by the death of his wife, are of the graveyard school; two commemorate national events (the entrance of Texas into the Union and the founding of Jamestown); two are satiric denunciations of public figures (N. P. Willis and John Jacob Astor); and one is a religious meditation in blank verse. The most vigorous and pointed of these is the denunciation of Astor, with the best part of the poem being its title: "On the death of J . . . J . . . . A . . . . who after a long life of meanness, trickery, and overreaching, died with several millions, leaving a large legacy to a Public Library, in consequence of which he was lauded to the skies for his liberality." The poem was never published.

In 1886 James Grant Wilson asserted, "Paulding himself was no poet."[33] To date, this observation has remained unchallenged, but somewhat inaccurate. The forgotten originality and vitality of *The Backwoodsman* argue for considerable qualification of the usual disclaimer.

Chapter Five

Literary Criticism

Paulding's nationalism, so prominent in his contributions to the Paper War, made him eminently suited for his role as a leader in the campaign for a national American literature that developed after the War of 1812. In the years following the Revolution and America's successful struggle for political independence, a few American writers such as Charles Brockden Brown and Royall Tyler in prefaces and prologues to their works had expressed the need for achieving American literary independence; however, it was only after the War of 1812 had awakened the national consciousness and given all Americans confidence in the strength of their nation, that the problem of literary nationalism attracted widespread attention and discussion.[1] Because of his love of American and hatred of England, Paulding insisted, more strongly than any of his contemporaries, that the problem was solvable and that American literature could free itself of foreign influence and become original and distinctly American, rather than merely English literature written in America. Furthermore, this insistence went far beyond chauvinistic boasting; throughout his life he pondered the nature and quality of American poetry, American drama, and American fiction, proposing in his literary criticism specific ways and means of cultivating originality, and attempting in his own works to provide useful examples for the more talented writers he was confident would follow him.

In *The United States and England,* which appeared on December 21, 1814,[2] Paulding first discussed the "peculiar difficulties" American writers faced in establishing "a distinct and characteristic national literature": the lack of a native language and habitual contemplation of English authors. These "difficulties have not yet been altogether overcome," he writes, "but they assuredly must be, and the victory will be one of the noblest ever achieved by human genius."[3] Not all American commentators on the nation's literary future agreed. Nine months later, in an article in the newly founded *North American*

Review, Walter Channing expressed what would become the conservative Federalist response to the problem of literary nationalism during the coming years. Channing, too, traced the reasons "for the barrenness of American Literature" to the lack of a native language and the popularity of foreign literature, but he explained that America's Colonial past had determined that "it must wait for all improvements from abroad, acquire a literary tone from the mother country, and like the civil jurisprudence of India, should it be as original in literature as they may be in crime, it must wait for a decision on its merits or demerits from the higher authorities of London." In a second article two months later, Channing pointed out what he saw as another major problem for the American writer: the poverty of American literary materials. "We are destitute of many of the elements of literature," he declared, adding, "we want a remote antiquity. . . . we want a vast variety of topicks of the very first interest in literature."[4]

During 1815–1825, the *North American Review* group ardently supported nationalism in American letters, often suggesting American subjects suitable for literary treatment; however, unlike Paulding, they praised the English literary tradition and voiced persistent doubts about the possibility of achieving a national literature of any originality or value.[5] Thus in 1818, when Paulding declared in his Preface to *The Backwoodsman* that the object of his experiment was to show young writers the "rich poetic resources" of America and to "call their attention *home*, for the means of attaining to novelty of subject," his words were informed by dissatisfaction with the tenacious acceptance of America's literary dependence upon England and by a prophetic insight into the means by which America could, and would, achieve an original national literature.

Because works such as *The Scarlet Letter* (1850), *Moby-Dick* (1851), *Leaves of Grass* (1855), and *The Adventures of Huckleberry Finn* (1884) are so familiar and so thoroughly American, we sometimes forget that, as late as 1820, the struggle for an authentic American literature was just beginning and there were few American writers of the day bold enough to experiment with American materials or themes. Scott, Byron, the Gothic romancers, and their imitators dominated the marketplace, and Cooper had only to his credit *Precaution* (1820), a novel of manners set in England, purporting to have been written by an Englishman. In 1820 Samuel Goodrich, the Boston publisher, estimated that three-fourths of the books Americans bought were of English origin, and it was in January of that same year that Sydney Smith in the *Edinburgh* sarcastically but justifiably asked, "Who reads an American book?"

Although Irving's *The Sketch Book* (1820) would contravene Smith's charges by becoming the first work by an American to receive international acclaim, Irving made little effort (except by writing Americanized versions of German folk tales) to encourage the establishment of an original American literature. On the contrary, in the essay of *The Sketch Book* entitled "English Writers on America," he declared, "We are a young people, necessarily an imitative one, and must take our examples and models, in a great degree, from the existing nations of Europe. There is no country more worthy of our study than England."[6]

It was in response to this sense of inferiority at home and condescension from abroad then that Paulding, in essays, reviews, prefaces, book chapters, and letters, wrote a formidable body of literary criticism concerned with advancing American literature toward independence. A letter to the editor of the *Southern Literary Messenger* starkly displays the standards of Paulding's criticism and reveals the distance separating his views from Irving's. "If your young writers," he wrote, "will consult their own taste and genius, and forget there ever were such writers as Scott, Byron, and Moore, I will be bound they produce something original; and a tolerable original is as much superior to a tolerable imitation, as a substance is to a shadow. Give us something new—something characteristic of yourselves, your country, and your native feelings, and I don't care what it is . . . I want to see something wholesome, natural, and national. The best thing a young American writer can do, is to forget that any body ever wrote before him" (*Letters*, 149).

Although Paulding's letter boldly and baldly presents the main criteria (i.e., originality, nationality, wholesomeness, and naturalness) underlying all of his literary criticism, it falls short of revealing the many qualifications and elaborations that distinguish his best critical essays. For example, in his essay-review "York Town: An Historical Romance," he qualifies his insistence upon originality by declaring that "a general acquaintance and familiarity with English literature, is of the greatest advantage to a young American writer, in forming his taste, and enlarging the sphere of his knowledge and perceptions;

but an abject imitation of any particular work, or any particular writer, if it does not bespeak inferiority, is pretty sure to create it in the end."[7] He then forcefully argues that imitation

> debilitates the mind, by furnishing its sole aliment, and thus rendering exertion unnecessary; it is feeding the grown up urchin with a spoon, when he should be taxing his energies to supply his own wants; it is surrendering a portion of intellectual independence, and colonizing our minds to writers, who, however they may assimilate in their opinions, can never be quite identified with ourselves. . . . No foreign writer can . . . speak so directly to the feelings and comprehension of the people of the United States, as one nurtured among them, partaking equally in the same original peculiarities, and standing in precisely the same situation with themselves, in relation to the subjects of which he treats. (30–31)

Unfortunately, the literary criticism that surfaces in Paulding's longer works tends to be, like that in his letter to the *Southern Literary Messenger,* superficial and intentionally provocative. In *A Sketch of Old England*, for example, he spends some one-hundred pages surveying the British literary scene, in the process characterizing Scott as "a capital pencil in copying old pictures, and colouring them afresh," Wordsworth and the lake-school poets as creators of "affected simplicity, sentimental ignorance, and simpering childishness," and Byron and his followers as specialists in "unbridled lust and unrestrained revenge."[8] Such comments, marred by "gall and bitterness," as Paulding later admitted and regretted, deserve only passing notice, for they reveal little about his contribution to Amercan critical thought. It is in his shorter critical pieces, especially his essay "National Literature" and his review-articles "American Drama" and "York Town," that one discovers evidence of a serious and acute critical mind at work.

"National Literature"

In his eight-page essay "National Literature" (which first appeared as an introduction to "The Wreck of Genius" in the September 2, 1820, issue of *Salmagundi, Second Series*), Paulding presents what Amos L. Herold has accurately described as a "comprehensive, credible, and original" theory of fiction.[9] In the first half of the essay, he rejects the widely held idea that American history and lore afford few materials for romantic fiction, calling it "without the shadow of a foundation." The idea, found not only in the criticism of the *North American Review*, but also in the lamentations of American writers who struggled with native subjects, was considered sound throughout much of the nineteenth century, as evidenced by its expression in Cooper's *Notions of the Americans* (1828), Hawthorne's Preface to the *Marble Faun* (1860), and James's biography *Hawthorne* (1879). In his essay Paulding defends America as a source of literary material by proposing a theory of realistic fiction, which draws upon the neoclassical belief that art should imitate nature and which anticipates the case for literary realism advanced by Howells, Twain, and James after the Civil War.[10] In two of the most important paragraphs of the essay, he explains that

> Wherever there are men, there will be materials for romantic adventure. In the misfortunes that befall them; in the sufferings and vicissitudes which are everywhere the lot of human beings; in the struggles to counteract fortune, and in the conflicts of the passions, in every situation of life, he who studies nature and draws his pictures from her rich and inexhaustible sources of variety, will always find enough of those characters and incidents which give a relish to works of fancy. The aid of superstition, the agency of ghosts, fairies, goblins, and all that antiquated machinery which till lately was confined to the nursery, is not necessary to excite our wonder or interest our feelings. . . .
>
> The best and most perfect works of imagination appear to me to be those which are founded upon a combination of such characters as every generation of men exhibits, and such events as have often taken place in the world, and will again. Such works are only fictions, because the tissue of events which they record never perhaps happened in precisely the same train, and to the same number of persons, as are exhibited and associated in the relation. Real life is fraught with adventures, to which the wildest fictions scarcely afford a parallel; and it has this special advantage over its rival, that these events, however extraordinary, can always be traced to motives, actions, and passions, arising out of circumstances no way unnatural, and partaking of no impossible or supernatural agency. (2:265–66)

Although the 1850s have been cited as the period when "theories of fiction were only just being born,"[11] Paulding's 1820 statements reveal that one such theory was being delivered much earlier. Of course, the climax of the critical controversy between Realism and Romanticism did not occur until the 1880s and 1890s. Nevertheless, when Howells declared that "fidelity to experience and probability of motive are essential conditions of a great imaginative literature," when Twain declared that the personages in a tale must "be alive, except in the case of corpses" and should "confine themselves to possibilities and let miracles alone," and when James declared that "the only reason for the existence of a novel is that it does attempt to represent life,"[12] each was succinctly restating a critical principle Paulding had articulated some sixty years before.

In the second half of "National Literature," Paulding turns to the American writer and his potential subject matter, declaring that while America indeed lacks the raw materials for mere romances with their "machinery of ghosts, goblins, and fairies," its history affords other materials such as the character of the American pioneers, their motives, their courage, their perseverence, their adventures, and their contests with the Indians, all of which are "amply sufficient" for the creation "of those higher works of imagination which may be called Rational Fictions" (2:269).

These materials have only been partially used, he observes, because we have "debased the genius of this new world by making it the ape and tributary of that of the old" (2:269). He thus calls upon the American writer to reject British models and contribute to America's literary independence "by freeing himself from a habit of servile imitation; by daring to think and feel, and express his feelings; by dwelling on scenes and events connected with our pride and our affections; by indulging in those little peculiarities of thought, feeling, and expression which belong to every nation . . ." (2:270). He concludes by accurately predicting that "this country, is not destined to be always behind in the race of literary glory. The time will assuredly come, when that same freedom of thought and action, which has given such a spur to our genius in other respects, will achieve similar wonders in literature" (2:271). (In two paragraphs added in 1835, he then praises the fiction of Charles Brockden Brown.)

If the nationalistic ideas of Paulding's essay appear familiar to the modern reader, it is probably because he or she has encountered them in Emerson's "The American Scholar" (1837), Melville's review "Hawthorne and His Mosses" (1850), or Whitman's Preface to

Leaves of Grass (1855), but it is important to recognize, as these three writers did not, that Paulding had expressed them sixteen, thirty, and thirty-five years before they did.

Though rudimentary and unsophisticated compared to modern theories of fiction, "National Literature" is, as Alexander Cowie has said, "a remarkable document of the period."[13] Paulding's insistence that the best fiction deals with the essences of life, with the realities of place, of time, of human behavior, plus his belief that awareness of these realities was essential to the American writer's quest for independence and excellence, mark the beginning of a new, serious attitude toward the art of fiction in America.

Perhaps not coincidentally, soon after the appearance of Paulding's essay, James Fenimore Cooper published *The Spy* (1821) and *The Pioneers* (1823), both of which dealt with American scenes and events, achieved immediate popularity, and permanently changed the direction of American literary development. As G. Harrison Orians has pointed out, "the decade of the twenties thereupon saw the rise of cisatlantic themes in native productions to the virtual neglect of imported ingredients. Suddenly there dawned the realization that our native country opened up to the adventurous novelist a wide, untrodden field, replete with new material, which gave vast scope to the imagination."[14] Significantly, in his Preface to *The Pioneers*, the most realistic of the Leatherstocking tales, Cooper wrote: ". . . I have come to the conclusion, that the writer of a tale, who takes the earth for the scene of his story, is in some degree bound to respect human nature. Therefore I would advise any one, who may take up this book with the expectation of meeting gods and goddesses, spooks or witches, . . . to throw it aside at once, for no such interest will be found in any of its pages." The echo here of Paulding's "National Literature" suggests that Cooper, who honored Paulding, as previously mentioned, by placing four lines from *The Backwoodsman* on the title page of *The Pioneers*, may have been guided by Paulding's ideas and example at the start of his career as America's first best-selling novelist. During the 1820s, seven Cooper novels became the most widely read books in America immediately following their publication, and it was not until 1831 that a historical novel by another American, who likewise focused on the American scene, achieved the same status.[15] The novel was *The Dutchman's Fireside*, and the author, of course, Paulding.

"American Drama"

"National Literature" is Paulding's best-known piece of literary criticism, and its significance has not gone unnoticed by several modern scholars. Thomas F. O'Donnell, for example, has called it "one of the most forceful and perceptive pieces of criticism that America had yet produced," while Luther S. Mansfield has observed that it sounded "the keynote for most of Paulding's serious work."[16] Nevertheless, "National Literature" forms only part of Paulding's best criticism and taken alone does not indicate the range of his critical interests or the complexity of his critical thoughts. These can best be seen in the eleven anonymous review articles he contributed to the *American Quarterly Review* between March 1827 and December 1832. This body of criticism, nearly three-hundred pages in total length, includes one review of a British novel, one of an American novel, two of American plays, two of naval autobiographies, two of travel books, two of historical accounts, and one of a report on the proceedings of Parliament.[17] Of these eleven pieces, two, "American Drama" and "York Town: An Historical Romance," stand out as the best, revealing the fertile ground of observation, reading, and thought that underlay and nourished his literary nationalism.

"American Drama" (June 1827) is a twenty-seven-page analysis of the decline of the drama in America, containing specific recommendations for infusing it with vitality and literary worth. Although the drama in America eventually developed along the lines Paulding set out (with his own famous play *The Lion of the West* [1830] being one of the first to put his theories into practice), much of his criticism in the article still seems remarkably relevant when considered in relation to modern derivations of the stage play, such as the cinema and television.

In the first half of the article, Paulding discusses what he sees as the three main causes for the decline of the drama in both America and England: vitiated public tastes, irresponsible theater managers, and the star system. The people, he observes, "will relish nothing living, but horses, dogs, dromedaries, and elephants prancing in the midst of pasteboard pageantry, conflagrations, bombardments, springing of mines, blowing up of castles, and such like accumulations of awful nursery horrors."[18] Theater managers have contributed to this degradation of the stage, Paulding claims, by pampering bad taste instead of catering to good taste, with the result that "the more refined classes of society" have stopped attending the theater, which has of consequence fallen . . . into the occupation of those who relish 'Tom and Jerry' better than Shakespeare or Sheridan" (335). Occasionally the managers do "bring forward a legitimate drama for the purpose of exhibiting a *star*," he acknowledges, but it is usually one of "the standard plays of a better era" (335); hence, talented young playwrights are denied an outlet for their work.

The star system, according to Paulding, undermines the development of American drama in a more indirect way as well. Because the star dominates a production and receives all the attention, the supporting actors "have no motive for exertion." Consequently, playwrights feel hopeless about "seeing justice done to their productions by the actors" (336) and are forced to write only plays that display and accommodate one actor's talents. Ultimately, only the star profits, Paulding argues, and "every other part of the theatre," including the orchestra, the supporting cast, and the management itself, is impoverished.

Although Paulding's indictment of the star system may seem unduly harsh, it was not. As Arthur Hobson Quinn has pointed out, many of the stars of the New York stage of the time came from abroad and were indifferent alike to the plight of American playwrights and American supporting actors. Visiting British greats such as Edmund and Charles Kean, William Charles Macready, and Charles and Fanny Kemble performed only in their own plays and were disinclined to attempt new roles in new works. Furthermore, benefiting from the intense rivalry among American theater managers, they demanded and received for their performances exorbitant fees, which too often exceeded the gate receipts brought in. As Quinn observes, "surely human sympathy must go out to the members of the stock company who witnessed a star like Miss Lydia Kelly, taking her nightly sum in cash, before she left the stage, with the knowledge that the balance did not provide their own modest salaries."[19]

Not surprisingly, when Paulding in the second half of his article focuses on the needs of the American stage, literary nationalism again receives his primary emphasis. He begins by calling for a national drama, defining it as "not merely a class of dramatic productions written by Americans, but one appealing directly to the national feelings; founded upon domestic incidents—illustrating or satirizing domestic manners—and, above all, displaying a generous chivalry in the maintenance and vindication of those great and illustrious peculiarities of situation and character, by which we are distinguished from all other nations" (339).

With this definition, Paulding seems guilty of what Quinn has called "the critical stupidity which followed foreign standards in expecting that [the American playwright] limit his themes to his own country, a standard never demanded of any other race";[20] however, it is not the themes or even the subject matter that comprise the essence of Paulding's definition. His main concern was that American drama be relevant to the unique features of life in America. In a second review article on the American drama published some three years later, he clarifies this point by explaining: "It is not necessary to be always writing on national subjects, or illustrating our own history and manners. But we do think, that the literature of a new country; new in its existence, its institutions, and situation, ought to have a special reference to these circumstances. It is this reference which alone can give it originality, and maintain its claim to a national character."[21]

As in "National Literature," Paulding in "American Drama" supports his call for literary nationalism by rebutting the idea that America lacks materials for the native writer to draw upon. Citing numerous American character types, such as the frontier settler, the white hunter, the Indian, he insists that the main obstacle for the American playwright is not the lack of "sufficient varieties of characters," but rather "the habit of imitation" (341–42).

The most important point Paulding makes concerning the development of the American drama is its need to free itself from the "lofty, sonorous, and imposing" dialogue then fettering it. After quoting speeches from several plays at hand and criticizing their incoherent and bombastic blank verse, he cites a passage from Dunlap's *Father of an Only Child* (1806) to illustrate the realistic rendering of human speech he believes other American playwrights should emulate. After praising the "colloquial ease and sprightliness" of Dunlap's dialogue, he asserts that "wit, whim, and elegant badinage, require far more talent in a perfomer, than ranting, mouthing, starting, and slapping the stomach" (352), and suggests that the latter must give way to the former if the stage is to be rescued from vulgarity.

Viewed in retrospect, Paulding's criticism in "American Drama" seems sound and prescient. Although both the star system and a prevailing taste for theatricality and imported productions hindered the development of a quality native drama throughout the nineteenth century, by 1910 American playwrights such as Augustus Thomas and Clyde Fitch had begun to write realistic plays featuring characters, dialogue, and events based on everyday life in America, thus vitalizing the American stage, refining the tastes of theater audiences, and initiating the American realistic tradition, later enriched with psychological depth by the major expressionistic dramas of Eugene O'Neill, Tennessee Williams, and Arthur Miller.

In his own plays, as in his fiction, Paulding attempted to put his critical theories into practice, particularly those regarding character and language. One of his efforts, *The Lion of the West*, written in 1830, three years after "American Drama" appeared, achieved enormous popularity and demonstrated the validity of the critical advice he had offered American writers. Paulding began the play at the suggestion of James H. Hackett, an American star who shared his interest in founding a national drama, and the result was the first American play to feature the uncouth Kentucky frontiersman.[22] This character, Colonel Nimrod Wildfire, played by Hackett and modeled on David Crockett, fascinated the American public and subsequently became a main character type in American literature and folklore. Wildfire's speeches received particular attention because of Paulding's successful rendering of the frontiersman's humorous tall talk, a manner of speaking he had heard and recorded as early as 1817 when he published *Letters from the South*.[23] Through its portrayal of an original native character, endowed with the dialect and humor of the old Southwest, *The Lion of the West*, as Louis D. Owens has pointed out, "played an unquestionably important role in opening up the field of regional literature in this country for such writers as Twain, Harte, Cable, Jewett, and others who would follow after mid-century."[24]

"York Town"

While "National Literature" and "American Drama" directly present Paulding's critical theories and serve to illuminate both his own works and the development of American literature, his review article "York Town: An Historical Romance" (September 1827) owes its distinction to its judicious criticism of British writers and its detailed explanation of the rationale informing Paulding's critical standards. Lacking the forceful generalizations of "National Literature" and the telling observations of "American Drama," "York Town" nevertheless contains some of the most thoughtful and wise literary criticism Paulding wrote.

In the space of some twenty-eight pages, he presents: first, a summary of the development of British literature, focusing on the political sentiments of major writers since the period of the first American settlements; second, a brief critique of the particular American historical romance under consideration; and third, a discussion of the principles that should be adopted by American writers of poetry and fiction. Throughout, his thesis is again the need for an original American literature, but here his supporting argument remains free from the bias and oversimplification often accompanying it in his other critical works.

Paulding begins by observing that the United States has repressed its own peculiar spirit by a habit of imitation, which originated during its colonial existence. He then implies that while the nation eventually acquired political principles and social ideals distinct from, and in fact antithetical to, those of the mother country, the habit of imitation persisted, particularly in our literary works. With this introduction he proceeds to examine British writings "peculiarly applicable to the state of this country, and its republican bias" (21), integrating his examination with a survey of British political developments from the sixteenth century to the present. Of the twenty-three writers he singles out for discussion, such as Spenser, Milton, Shakespeare, Dryden, Pope, and so on, most receive evenhanded treatment. His discussion of Shakespeare's political sentiments, which offended him, is an example of the fairmindedness displayed in the essay as a whole. At first, his republican sympathies govern his criticism as he emphasizes Shakespeare's subservience to James I and his ridicule of the lowborn in his plays. The discussion concludes, however, with the judgment that

> For this, not Shakespeare, but the age in which he lived is answerable. It could never have been in the nature of such a divine genius, to become the flatterer of kings, and the contemner of the people, had not the ex-

ample of all around, and of the very people themselves, obliged him to stoop to this degradation. Had Shakespeare lived in these times, there can be little reason to doubt, that the universal example, now so different, would have encouraged him to a different course, and led him to do justice to the more liberal conceptions of his mighty mind. (26).

Even in his discussions of contemporary British writers, whom he had even less reason or inclination to admire, Paulding offers judicious evaluations that have stood the test of time. Wordsworth, for example, whom he had ridiculed in *A Sketch of Old England*, here is credited with"genius," which "has been, in a great measure, employed in giving dignity and importance to the passions and incidents of ordinary life" (29). More surprisingly, Scott, whom Paulding had parodied, satirized, ridiculed, and condemned in six volumes over the course of fifteen years, also receives commendation. While Paulding observes that no one would attribute to Scott republican sympathies, he also acknowledges Scott's respectful characterizations of commoners and identifies as strengths in his works "the easy, flowing, and natural style . . . , the clear conception, and happy discrimination of character; the rich unaffected sentiment; the beautiful descriptions of scenery; the animated action; and above all, the strong infusion of good manly sense, which gives dignity even to occasional extravagance" (34).

The point of Paulding's survey of British writers and works is to concede that "so long as it is our destiny to imitate, or to borrow our literature . . . we cannot perhaps resort to a better and purer source than England." He uses this concession, however, to gain support for his thesis, which he immediately turns toward with the observation that if the necessity to borrow or imitate "does really exist," it is "a mortifying, not to say injurious necessity" (30). In the manner shown earlier in this chapter, he then elaborates upon the debilitating effects of imitation, emphasizing that the distinct political histories of England and the United States have created an ideological chasm between their respective institutions that cannot be bridged by a common language. "When a sober and rational English writer talks of liberty," he explains, "he means not United States liberty. . . ." Rather, "he means distinctions of rank; an established church with exclusive privileges; a hereditary monarch; hereditary nobles; hereditary legislators; hereditary distinctions of every kind." Thus, no foreign writer, particularly an Englishman, can "speak so directly to the feelings and comprehensions of the people of the United States, as one nurtured among them" (31).

Having provided this rather complex rationale for the main idea of this article, Paulding states it explicitly: ". . . every nation ought, as soon as possible, to have a literature of its own, adapted to its peculiar situation; addressing itself, on all proper occasions, to the national feeling; and administering, either directly or indirectly, as the subject may warrant, to the support of the national honour" (31).

Paulding's achievement in the first half of "York Town" consists not only of his persuasive argument for an original American literature and his judicious treatment of British authors, but also of his skillful delineation of the central dilemma confronting the American writer at the time and for some thirty years to come. On the one hand, he had inherited from his own nation a political tradition essentially democratic in spirit and tone, which in 1827 had already begun to affect our social development, as Paulding points out, and would do so dramatically after the election of Jackson in the following year. On the other hand, from England he had inherited a literary tradition inextricably bound to aristocratic conventions in British society and politics. For years British writers, with the exceptions Paulding singles out for praise, either depended upon the aristocracy for patronage or belonged to it. In either case, they tended to perpetuate the myth of the gentleman author for whom writing was an avocation undertaken to please himself and members of his class rather than a vocation involving a mass audience. Lord Byron, who refused to accept money from the sale of his works, was one of the last to insist on the reality of the myth, but in America it continued to exert a powerful influence, affecting the tone, and often the content, of American works. Irving, Cooper, and later even Melville adopted the persona of the aristocratic amateur, while by necessity rejecting the unprofitable indifference to royalties it implied.

At the height of their careers, the five great American writers of mid-century—Emerson, Thoreau, Hawthorne, Melville, and Whitman—embraced the ideals of the American political tradition rather than those of the British literary one; nevertheless, with the exception of Whitman, none could completely reject the respect for birth, breeding, manners, rank, and class inculcated by British example. The idea of the common man, of equality, of fraternity, of democracy inspired them, but the reality often repulsed them. F. O. Matthiessen in his seminal study *American Renaissance* affirms the validity of Paulding's theory that American political principles would be the distinguishing features of a triumphant American literature, by pointing out that "the one common denominator" of the five major writers of the renaissance "was their devotion to the possibilities of democracy."[25] What Matthiessen does not stress, however, but what Paulding's discussion adumbrates, is that foreign influence often weakened this devotion; such examples as the curious conclusion of *The House of the Seven Gables* and the "majestical trappings and housings" of *Moby-Dick* indicate the persistent attraction of the British aristocratic tradition even as American writers were most ardently trying to affirm national political ideals.

Although originality and nationality (inseparable in Paulding's mind when applied to American literature) are the two critical standards receiving his most extensive development in "York Town," he also presents persuasive explanations of his other main standards, wholesomeness and naturalness. His insistence upon wholesomeness in literature originated in his neoclassical preference for simplicity, decorum, and moderation, and he most often applied it when criticizing the sensational immorality and violence of first the Gothic novel and later the sentimental romance. In 1849, for example, it informed his indictment of the prevailing taste for "high seasoned dishes of foreign cookery, most especially blood-puddings, plentifully spiced and sauced with adultery, seduction, poisoning, stabbing, suicide, and all other sublime excesses of genius."[26] In "York Town," on the other hand, it surfaces in his discussion of the poetry of Moore and Byron, which he charges respectively with "epigrammatic voluptuousness" and "deep sentimental Eastern voluptuousness," the latter he claims, sometimes displaying itself "in lofty heroics," "grovelling intrigue," and "naked sensuality" (29).

Unlike Howells, who would argue for wholesomeness by declaring that violence and "vicious love" were inappropriate subjects for young girls to read about and were uncharacteristic of contemporary society, which he saw growing more decent, Paulding offers a rationale neither prudish nor naïve. "We are not of those," he writes, "who hold that every poem ought to be a moral essay, or that we should find 'sermons in stones,' as we walk the streets. Much less do we think that dulness is deified by being very orthodox" (29). He goes on to say that whereas an author is not responsible for the morality of his characters or their actions, "nothing but a bad taste, or a corrupt fancy, would indulge itself in the pleasure of representing triumphant guilt as an object of admiration, or stimulating the passions by luxurious pictures of licentious love" (29). Paulding, of course, recognized that immorality is a very real part of life, and he admits that "under the influence of actual and immediate temptation, and when assailed by the seductions of sense, there may be some excuse for yielding." He adds, however, that to think immorally in our closets, and then commit the overt act of obtruding these thoughts upon the world, is to become practically as well as abstractedly wicked; it is a voluntary and gratuitous species of turpitude, similar to that of a person who commits a crime without the excuse of temptation" (29–30). Paulding's underlying assumptions here are that the writer should have some moral vision that can guide the reader's response to a character's actions, and he should not present sensational material merely for its own sake, assumptions now shared by some, but of course not all, of our contemporary writers.

Paulding's argument for naturalness in "York Town" elaborates upon the theory of Rational Fictions he presented in "National Literature." Again he insists that fiction, particularly historical romance, should show a "close adherence to Nature, which is but another name for Truth" (46). He here develops this idea, which he encountered in Fielding, by explaining why the supernatural should particularly be excluded from historical fiction dealing with the United States and why for other times and places, it may be appropriate for inclusion. "Strictly speaking," he writes, "there has been no dark or romantic age, in this country, connected with its European race. The adventures, the sufferings, the conflicts, of our forefathers, besides being of a recent date, all partook of severe reality" (42). Having cited the belief in witchcraft as the only exception to this generalization (an exception that Hawthorne, too, noticed well), he then elaborates upon the differences between our past and that of other countries, revealing that in the application of his standard of naturalness, a concern for psychological truth takes precedence over merely external and visible truth. "As the romance writer recedes from the present time," he writes "or the domestic sphere of action, he may indulge a greater latitude of improbability" (45). This is because the supernatural often constituted a believable reality for people of earlier ages. For example, "the early poets and romance writers of Europe," he explains, "exhibit a strange mixture of Christian and Pagan supernatural agency in their works, because the human mind may be said to have been in those days, pretty much in the situation of the Holy Land, where the Infidel and the Christian were struggling for mastery." Likewise, "the Pagan system is recognized and admired in the ancients, because, although we do not believe in it, we know that they did. It was sublime in them—it would be ridiculous in us" (43–44).

The sophistication and flexibility of Paulding's rationale for naturalness is apparent when one considers that such improbable fictions as "Young Goodman Brown" and *The Scarlet Letter*, whose characters believe in the reality of the supernatural, would be judged fairly and favorably if the standard were applied to them. The same, of course, would be true for the later realistic works of Howells, James, and Twain, although the improbabilities at the end of *The Adventures of Huckleberry Finn* would stand out as major weaknesses, which, of course, most modern critics judge them to be.

Paulding's best criticism then, not only in "York Town," but also in "American Drama" and "National Literature," seems to verify Amos L. Herold's observation that he "was a literary theorist equalled by few and perhaps surpassed by none of his fellow writers."[27] Unfortunately, because a number of his important critical writings were published anonymously, studies of the development of American literary criticism have failed to recognize the extent of his achievement. For example, William Charvat's *The Origins of American Critical Thought, 1810–1835*, still the standard work on its subject, declares that "In spite of its literary atmosphere, New York did not do distinguished work in criticism. . . . Irving and Paulding wrote little important criticism, and the Knickerbocker Magazine group belongs in the next period."[28] Thanks to the work of Ralph M. Aderman, who has identified Paulding's contributions to American magazines, it is now ironically apparent that Charvat himself unknowingly argued for Paulding's distinction and importance as a critic.

In his chapter on the criticism of poetic technique, Charvat credits one anonymous critic in the *Analectic* with understanding and expressing "the modern idea of images for their own sake."[29] The critic was Paulding. In his chapter on the criticism of the drama, he credits the *American Quarterly Review* with making the only "serious attempt to keep up with contemporary plays" and being "the first important periodical to call for a national drama."[30] The anonymous reviews he cites as support were written by Paulding. Finally, in his chapter on the criticism of fiction, he overlooks Paulding's "National Literature," but quotes an anonymous review that advised American writers on the use of native materials and another that warned them against their tendency to ape Scott.[31] Both of the reviews were written by Paulding.[32]

Chapter Six

Plays

Paulding's love and knowledge of the theater, so clearly revealed in his criticism of the drama, undoubtedly inspired his own playwriting efforts and accounted in part for the popular success he achieved with *The Lion of the West*, the second of four plays he wrote. In "American Drama" he revealed his own qualifications as a playwright when he observed that successful plays were most often written by those "who by a long habit of hanging about the theatres, associating with actors, and observing what takes with a majority of the audience, have acquired a knack, a facility in laying traps for applause, and actually forcing occasions for laughter or surprise" (354). His "hanging about" apparently began as soon as he arrived in New York City at about the age of eighteen, for we know that he accompanied his young friend Irving, then about thirteen, on his first surreptitious visit to the theater, where the two saw the comedy *Speculation*.[1] When Irving subsequently made a habit of sneaking off to performances against his father's wishes, Paulding certainly joined him, and in time both became inveterate theatergoers.

As his criticism reveals, Paulding eventually became disenchanted with the contemporary theater, particularly its failure to present American plays dealing with the unique features of American life; he therefore tried to bring about a change. His Preface to the volume containing his first play, *The Bucktails* (written soon after the War of 1812 and published in 1847), echoes the Preface to *The Backwoodsman* in its emphasis on the author's intent to provide an example for other American writers. Observing that America has no drama "based on our own manners, habits, character and political institutions," he states that the "foundation must be laid, however weak and unfinished, and a hope, not indeed very sanguine, is entertained that this experiment may at least be sufficiently successful to stimulate others better qualified to excel in this rather neglected species of literature" (iii–iv). Although this particular play failed to achieve the result

Paulding hoped for, the second play he wrote eventually did, for in the seventeen years between the writing of *The Bucktails* and the writing of *The Lion of the West*, Paulding developed his theories about the essential features of an original American drama and improved upon his ability to put these theories into practice. We do not know whether he continued to improve as a playwright, however, for his third and fourth plays, with the unpromising titles of *Fanaticism and Hypocrisy* (a tragedy) and *Sea Nymph* (a dramatic romance), apparently written in the early 1830s and intended for inclusion in the last volume of the 1835 edition of his collected works,[2] were never published, and their contents and fates remain unknown.

The Bucktails

The Bucktails, or Americans in England is a five-act comedy of manners containing some amusing American humor that is its chief asset. It was never staged, but in 1846 Paulding informed his publishers that it "was Several Years ago in Rehearsal at the Philadelphia Theatre, under the direction of Messrs. Warren & Wood, just at the period the establishment became Insolvent, and I have never Since offered it either for publication or performance" (*Letters*, 433). Although Amos L. Herold has declared the play "both readable and actable," a more accurate estimate was given by Evert A. Duyckinck, who criticized its plot as defective, and its incidents as insufficiently dramatic.[3]

The first two acts, especially, move very slowly, and in them little is accomplished other than the introduction of fifteen characters, many of whom, such as Obsolete, Rust, Threadneedle, and Gunwale, are borrowed from eighteenth-century comedies of humours and have eccentricities in accordance with their names. The setting is London, and what plot there is revolves around a dinner party planned by Obsolete, an English Antiquarian, for two newly arrived Americans, Henry and Frank Tudor. The main source of humor derives from the absurd preconceptions the English characters have about the Tudor brothers. Miss Obsolete, as mentioned in chapter 3, is shocked that her brother has invited them and says she has been assured that Americans are "aboriginals" who wear rings in their noses, eat raw meat, paint their faces outlandishly, and go about half naked. When the Tudors arrive, of course, they are not wild aboriginals with bucktails, but kind and cultured gentlemen, and after they mix with the company, a romantic interest develops between them and the two young ladies present, Jane Warfield, an American heiress living in London, and Mary Obsolete, the antiquarian's daughter.

In act 3, Paulding generates some successful low comedy in the exchanges between Jonathan Peabody, the Tudors' servant, and his English counterparts, Rust and Paddy Whack. Also, an after-dinner conversation between Henry Tudor and Miss Obsolete concerning Yankee notions of courting contains entertaining wit. Nevertheless, it is only at the end of the act that the plot thickens slightly for the first time when Lord Noland, a profligate, declares of Jane: "I must either make her love me, or run away with her, and make her a lady against her will" (56).

The pace of the play picks up considerably in act 4, as Henry Tudor successfully proposes to Jane, who is then abducted by a band of ruffians in the employ of Noland. In act 5, she escapes, and three parties roam at night through a forest looking for her, two attempting to save her, the third to recapture and deflower her. In the most lively scene of the act, Jane, pale and fatigued, enters a church graveyard where Jonathan, mistaking her for a ghost, shoots at her; she then flees to an old ruined castle where she encounters a band of gypsy beggars gathered around a fire. At this point, however, instead of accelerating toward a climax, the play comes to a standstill, as Paulding has the King of the gypsies play the wit and deliver a number of gratuitous satiric observations on the English political system. Eventually though, everyone arrives, Noland is foiled, Jane is saved, Mary accepts Frank's proposal of marriage, and the Tudor brothers make plans to return to the New World with their fiancées.

With its weak plot, derivative characters, and tiresome dialogue, *The Bucktails* does not qualify as outstanding drama; nevertheless, it is amusing in places, and as Floyd C. Watkins has pointed out, its best humor arises from the character of Jonathan, a mixture of frontiersman and New Englander, who is "the first stage character to discuss his frontier and animal blood,"[4] as he does when he declares, "I'm half horse, half alligator, and a little of the *Ingen*, I guess" (81). Jonathan also exhibits American peculiarities of character through his dialect and comic blend of naiveté and shrewdness. Lost in the streets of London, for example, he declares, "What tarnal comical creturs these towns are. I'll be darned but I guess I've lost my way, though I chalked the corners of the streets as I went along" (33–34). Similarly, when he encounters a London Hackney coachman and asks the way home, the following dialogue takes place:

Coachman:	This fellow is a real bumpkin—I'll quiz him. What's your name, friend?
Jonathan:	Name? Why darnation how should I know? Do you think I stood my own godfather?
Coachman:	The fellow's a perfect natural. Maybe you can tell who owns the house you stay at, friend.
Jonathan:	O yes! the man that lives in it, I partly guess.
Coachman:	A bright guess—who lives in it, then?
Jonathan:	He that owns it, like as not. (34)

The coachman finally tries to trick Jonathan by giving him false directions, but Jonathan responds in kind, sending the coachman rushing off to meet a fictitious gentleman supposedly waiting for him and his coach. Admittedly, the scene and several others like it do not constitute uproarious comedy, but they demonstrate Paulding's budding skill at creating a native comic type that would reappear in more robust and delightful form in his second play, *The Lion of the West.*

The Lion of the West

In early 1830 when James H. Hackett, the popular American comedian, offered a $300 prize for "an original comedy whereof an American should be the leading character,"[5] he encouraged Paulding to compete, and in December 1830 the judges, who included William Cullen Bryant and Fitz-Greene Halleck, selected Paulding's *The Lion of the West; or a Trip to Washington* as the best submission. Paulding obviously wrote the play with his critical dicta in mind, and the *New-York Mirror* in its announcement of the award appropriately praised his "noble ambition to second the efforts of our indigenous comedian in laying the foundation for a national drama."[6]

The hero of the drama, Colonel Nimrod Wildfire, played by Hackett, is a wild Kentucky frontiersman, "half horse and half alligator," who boasts he can "jump higher—squat lower—dive deeper—stay longer under and come out drier" than "all the fellers on this side the Alleghany mountains."[7] Paulding based this character upon the colorful congressman from Tennessee, David Crockett, and was indebted to John Wesley Jarvis, portrait painter and raconteur par excellence, for much of his material about him.[8] Sometime in 1830, Paulding asked Jarvis to furnish him with "a few sketches, short stories & incidents, of Kentucky or Tennessee manners, and especially some of their peculiar phrases & comparisons." He also asked that Jarvis "add, or *invent* a few ludicrous Scenes of Col. Crockett at Washington" (*Letters*, 113).

When the play was about to be staged, rumors of Paulding's caricature of Crockett circulated in the newspapers, and he felt compelled to deny them publicly in the *New-York Mirror* and privately in a letter to Crockett, whose goodnatured response makes Paulding's lie seem quite unattractive by contrast:

Washington City. 22nd Decr. 1830

Sir your letter of the 15 Inst was handed to me this day by my friend Mr. Wilde—the newspaper publications to which you refer I have never seen; and if I had I should not have taken the reference to myself in exclusion of many who fill offices and who are as untaught as I am. I thank you however for your civility in assuring me that you had no reference to my peculiarities. The frankness of your letter induces me to say a declaration from you to that effect was not necessary to convince me that you were incapable of wounding the feelings of a strainger and unlettered man who had never injured you—your character for letters and as a gentleman is not altogather unknown to me.

I have the honor with
great respects &c—
DAVID CROCKETT[9]

Despite Paulding's protestations and Crockett's gracious acceptance, the public persisted in identifying Crockett as the model for Wildfire, and Crockett himself encouraged it, inviting Hackett to bring the play to Washington, where from his front-row seat he stood and exchanged bows with Hackett, on stage as Wildfire, to the spectators' delight.[10]

Hackett's long run of performances of *The Lion of the West* began on April 25, 1831, at the Park Theater in New York City, and although it drew enthusiastic full houses and favorable reviews, Hacket apparently thought it needed revision, for in the summer of 1831 he commissioned the playwright John Augustus Stone to rewrite it.[11] In September the *New-York Mirror* reported favorably on the new version and observed that Stone had "arranged an entire new piece, with the exception of Wildfire."[12]

From the fall of 1831 through the fall of 1832, the revised play was warmly received in cities throughout the United States, including Boston, Philadelphia, New York, Charleston, and Cincinnati. During this period Mrs. Frances Trollope's infamous travel book *Domestic Manners of the Americans*, published in England in March 1832, was creating a stir in America because of its scathing attack on almost all things American, and before Hackett performed the play in London in March 1833, a caricature of Mrs. Trollope (named Mrs. Amelia Wallope), plus some biting satire directed at her analysis of Americans, was written into the play. Joyce Henry has argued convincingly that the author of the revisions was Paulding himself and that five anonymous "Leaves from Mrs. Trollope's Journal" that appeared in the *New-York Mirror* in the summer of 1832 were his as well.[13]

The version of *The Lion of the West* performed in London was entitled *The Kentuckian; or, a Trip to New York in 1815*, and in the manuscript licensed by the Lord Chamberlain's Office (the only extant copy of the play), the British playwright William Bayle Bernard is credited with revising it. Alterations evident in the manuscript itself are the deletions of expletives, the substitution of the name Mrs. Luminary for Mrs. Wollope, and the elimination of all references to *Domestic Manners of the Americans*, including indirect references such as the word *manners*.[14] Because Bernard never claimed rights to the play, Henry has suggested that he did not rewrite the play, but merely made the alterations cited above. If this was the case, then Paulding was the author of the unaltered third version, which was probably the one that Hackett performed successfully in the United States for many years after returning from England. In about 1860, he informed Paulding's son William that the play had been a hit in London and that later he had "repeatedly acted the character in that drama in every principal city of the U. States with applause, and in every theatrical engagement I made for twenty years following."[15]

Until James N. Tidwell discovered the manuscript of *The Lion of the West* in the British Museum in 1951, it was considered "lost," for neither Paulding's son nor twentieth-century scholars could locate a copy of it. The comedy as we now have it, edited by Tidwell and published by Stanford University Press, is a farce in two acts, with the main plot dealing with the competition between two Englishmen for the hand of Caroline Freeman, the daughter of a prosperous New York merchant. Of the two suitors, Mr. Percival, a good-hearted young merchant, is the favorite of Caroline and her father, while an imposter named Jenkins, calling himself Lord Grandby, is the choice of Caroline's social-climbing mother. The more engaging subplot involves Caroline's cousin Nimrod Wildfire, the wild Kentucky Colonel, and his infatuation with Mrs. Amelia Wollope, Jenkins's widowed sister, who is visiting America to gather material for her book *Domestic Manners of the Americans.*

The play moves at a rapid, efficient pace and includes a number of visual treats, such as Wildfire's buckskin jacket and wildcat cap,[16] his furious after-dinner jig that sends the refreshments flying, the preparation for a rifle duel between him and a reluctant Jenkins, and a stagecoach ride across the back of the stage by a screaming Mrs. Wollope, who has been mistakenly abducted by Jenkins's men. The characters' personalities as well as their actions yield many comic moments, and, as in Henry James's *The American*, the triumph of American honesty, candor, and goodwill over European meanness, deceit, and pretentiousness forms the thematic heart of the work.

Colonel Wildfire and Mrs. Wollope embody the two sets of traits most clearly, and, as Melvin R. Mason has pointed out, the interaction between these characters "accounts for the basic appeal of the play."[17] Amelia Wollope, like her prototype Frances Trollope, exudes disdain for the scene of her "experiment." When she arrives at the City Hotel in act 1, she quickly declares that "to ameliorate the barbarism of manners in America has been the ruling wish of my life. . . . The root of all the evil of this country is familiarity—where every one is equal, every one is familiar" (31). As she helps her brother carry out his plan of deception and abduction, she humorlessly notes and sketches the worst examples of American manners she finds, and Wildfire, of course, provides her with many.

In act 1, Wildfire, hearing of her project, visits her at the hotel to offer information, and being told that a card is called for, he sends in the king of clubs. After he enters, he draws up two chairs, sits on one, and puts his feet on the other. As Mrs. Wollope listens amazed, he then tells his tall tale about Kentucky soil being so rich that he once found a hat floating in the swamp, and when he lifted it with his whip, "a feller sung out from under it, Hallo stranger, who told you to knock my hat off, . . . I'm doing beautifully—got one of the best horses under me that ever burrowed—claws like a mole." "This," responds Mrs. Wollope, "shall be the first well authenticated anecdote in my perusal" (35–36).

By act 2, Mrs. Wollope has acquired private disdain for the Colonel, but she solicits funds from him for a national social academy and asks him to accompany her to the spot of her "future home in America." He misunderstands her intentions, however, and makes plans to whisk her off to "Old Kaintuck" as his bride. "I have ordered a good strong covered waggon for the journey," he writes her. "There's a parson close by who hitches teams quicker than any feller in the country. I'll go fetch him by the collar in less than a flash. In five minutes we two will be hammered into one . . ." (45). After reading this aloud, Mrs. Wollope declares, "Marry me and carry me in a covered waggon to the backwoods! The stupid, ignorant, familiar brute—does he think for a moment I could waste a thought—the supposition is an insult! This must be ameliorated!" (45–46).

When Jenkins arrives and tells her that talk of pistols will scare Wildfire off, Mrs. Wollope replies, "Then, my dear brother, shoot him instantly" (49), but when the Colonel receives Jenkins's challenge, he is elated, declaring to Percival, "I always go primed for such fun!" To show what he means, he tells the following classic tall tale worth quoting in its entirety:

I was riding along the Mississippi one day when I came across a fellow floating down the stream sitting cock'd up in the starn of his boat fast asleep. Well, I hadn't had a fight for as much as ten days—felt as though I must kiver myself up in a salt bin to keep—"so wolfy" about the head and shoulders. So, says I, hullo, stranger, if you don't take keer your boat will run away wi' you. So he looked up at me "slantindickular," and I looked down on him "slanchwise." He took out a chaw of tobacco from his mouth and, says he, I don't value you tantamount to that, and then he flopp'd his wings and crowed like a cock. I ris up, shook my mane, crooked my neck, and neighed like a horse. Well, he run his boat foremost ashore. I stopped my waggon and set my triggers. Mister, says he, I'm the best man—if I ain't, I wish I may be tetotaciously exflunctified! I can whip my weight in wild cats and ride strait through a crab apple orchard on a flash of lightning—clear meat axe disposition! And what's more, I once back'd a bull off a bridge. Poh, says I, what do I keer for that? I can tote a steam boat up the Mississippi and over the Alleghany

> mountains. My father can whip the best man in old Kaintuck, and I can whip my father. When I'm good natured I weigh about a hundred and seventy, but when I'm mad, I weigh a *ton*. With that I fetched him the regular Ingen war-whoop. Out he jumped from his boat, and down I tumbled from my waggon—and, I say, we came together like two steam boats going sixty mile an hour. He was a pretty severe colt, but no part of a priming to such a feller as me. I put it to him mighty droll—tickled the varmint till he squealed like a young colt, bellowed "enough" and swore I was a "rip staver." Says I, *ain't* I a horse? Says he, stranger, you're a *beauty* anyhow, and if you'd stand for Congress I'd vote for you next *lection*. Says I, would you? My name's Nimrod Wildfire. Why, I'm the yaller flower of the forest. I'm all *brimstone but* the *head*, and that's *aky fortis*. (54–55)

Soon after the telling of this tale, the duel begins, with Wildfire prepared to "blaze away like a thunder cloud" (60), but before he can, Jenkins exposes himself as a coward and Mr. Freeman arrives with information exposing him as a fraud. Meanwhile, Percival rescues Mrs. Wollope from an abduction intended for Caroline, and Mr. Freeman, speaking for Paulding, tells her, "I regret to inform you, madam, that our inhabitants are unfavorable to your design. . . . It is their opinion that as refinement in all countries has been the result of wealth and leisure, America must provide for her wants before she can be in a condition to welcome those who would increase her luxuries" (61). At the end of the play then, Mrs. Wollope vows to return to England with her "observations," while Wildfire gives to Percival and Caroline as a wedding gift some of his Kentucky property where "the ground's so rich . . . that if you but plant a crowbar over night *perhaps* it will sprout tenpenny nails afore mornin' " (62).

The Lion of the West, as mentioned in chapter 5, possesses historical importance, for it was the first drama to feature a native American type, the frontiersman, who has since become a central figure in American folklore. Propagators of the Crockett legend drew heavily upon Paulding's play, and, in fact, the author of the *Sketches and Eccentricities of Col. David Crockett of West Tennessee* (1833) incorporated Wildfire's longest yarn into his book with little alteration.[18] Perhaps just as important, however, is that Paulding's play is still a joy to read, retaining much of its freshness and high-spirited humor even after the passage of some 150 years.

Although there is an anti-intellectual bias in Paulding's humor, as there would be in much of the native American humor that would follow, his play does not challenge accepted notions of right and wrong or belong to the subversive tradition established by humorous works such as Alphonso Wetmore's play *The Pedlar* (1821), Johnson J. Hooper's *Simon Sugg's Adventures* (1845), or George W. Harris's *Sut Lovingood's Yarns* (1867).[19] In *The Lion of the West*, as in James's *The American* (1877; dramatized by the author in 1891), the most fundamental contrast underlying the comic encounters between the main characters is not one of manners, or education, or nationality, but rather one of morals, and at this level the play affirms, rather than subverts, conventional standards of decency and goodness.[20] As Paulding explained in a letter of 1813, which has direct relevance to his intentions in *Lion of the West*, southerners "are a most potent Set of roysterers, toss pots, and Barbecue villains . . . Yet do I like them, for there is a great generosity, gallantry, and frankness in their dispositions, and they have not that mean hypocrisy, and narrow selfishness which I beg leave to say is one of the precious 'Steady Habits' of New England" (*Letters*, 33–34). Although Wildfire is westerner rather than southerner and Wollope is English rather than New Englander, Paulding's respective sets of admiration and dislike came from the same perceptions. At its heart, then, the comedy of *The Lion of the West* is a celebration not of uncouthness, but of generosity of spirit, and as such the laughter it inspires is certainly worthy of enjoyment.

Chapter Seven

Short Stories

One can make a case either for or against Paulding as a writer of short fiction. On the negative side, he wrote some of the most unrealistic, rambling, trite, and trifling short works ever inflicted upon a literate public—and he wrote many of them. His short fiction can be categorized under numerous headings, including folktales, ghost stories, fables, frontier tales, fairy tales, love stories, allegories, Oriental tales, and satires, and if one suffers through a reading of the twenty-seven assorted pieces in the six collections of his short fiction and the seventy-three additional ones in Melvin Mason's three-volume dissertation, "The Uncollected Stories of James Kirke Paulding," it is difficult not to agree with one critic's assertion that Paulding's "short writings especially are sometimes as bad as anything published in America during his age."[1] Apparently Paulding had little respect for short fiction (which would not become an established genre until after his period of greatest productivity), and his motives for writing it were often less than noble. As Fred Lewis Pattee has observed, with partial accuracy, "To Paulding the tale was a journalistic form, a bid for cash and for literary popularity."[2]

On the positive side, Paulding occasionally experimented in earnest with the short-story form, using American materials with care and producing a handful of works that contributed to the foundation of an original American literature. Two of his stories of the New York Dutch, "The Little Dutch Sentinel of the Manhadoes" and "Cobus Yerks," are excellent, having sophisticated plots, believable characters, and rich local color, while three of his other stories, "The Dumb Girl," "Childe Roeliffe's Pilgrimage," and "The Adventures of Henry Bird," are only slightly less admirable.

Most of Paulding's stories appeared in periodicals such as the *New-York Mirror, Graham's Magazine*, and *Godey's Lady's Book*, but thirteen were published in the first literary annual, *The Atlantic Souvenir*, which initiated the gift-book craze that lasted for some thirty years. Expensive, lavishly illustrated, elegantly bound, *The Atlantic Souvenir*, like its imitators, was designed to appeal to the tastes of wealthy fashionable Americans, and it claimed to spare no expense to obtain the best specimens of American writing. Either because of its distinction or, as Amos L. Herold has suggested, because it allowed time for careful planning and composing,[3] the *Souvenir* garnered Paulding's best efforts, and both "The Little Dutch Sentinel" and "Cobus Yerks" first appeared on its beautiful pages.

"The Little Dutch Sentinel"

"The Little Dutch Sentinel of the Manhadoes" (1827) is the story of an impressionable little Dutchman whose sighting of a specter disrupts the town of New Amsterdam in the year 1670. Artful shifts in point of view and time sequence distinguish the structure of the tale, as Paulding has a young man named Egbert, the narrator, recall his grandfather, an old Dutchman named Aurie Doremus, who, as he sits on the porch of his little Dutch house in New York City in the year 1825, entertains his grandchildren with his reminiscences, which include the story of Jan Sol.

Long ago, Aurie relates, the citizens of New Amsterdam lived in fear of Indians, ghosts, and witches, and in 1670 they were additionally frightened by recent ominous signs, such as an outbreak of toadstools and the rattlings of invisible carriages at night. Every citizen of the small and vulnerable community took turns standing guard at night and in the daytime helped enforce the military code, which specified the death penalty for anyone going in or out of the fort except through the gate, which was shut from sundown to sunrise.

One summer moonlit night, as Jan Sol, a bandy legged little boaster, nervously stood watch, he saw on the river a canoe, which mysteriously disappeared. Moments later, he saw what he later swore was a gigantic specter, which appeared over the wall some one-hundred yards away directly in line with the windmill. It put forth an enormous pair of wings and, while its eyes flashed fire and its teeth glowed, it whirled in the air, then flew from the wall toward the Governor's garden and disappeared. The town, panicked by Jan's report, takes measures to detect the specter, but it does not appear again until the next Saturday, when Jan alone sees it again. One week later, a six-man guard, selected by the town council, stands watch fortified by strong drink. All but Jan fall asleep, however, and he again sees the specter, which flies toward the gate of the Governor's garden. The guards, awakened by Jan, pursue it, arousing the Governor and his only daughter Blandina, a pretty little Dutch damsel, and after a search, they apprehend a handsome young man who refuses to tell who he is or why he is there.

As the mystery of his identity is introduced, another is cleared up; the keeper of the windmill recalls that on the two nights Jan saw the specter, he had set his windmill going at the time of the sightings. Because the young man scaled the wall at a place in line with the windmill and the spot Jan held watch, his figure became identified with the wings of the mill.

After the prisoner is sentenced to death, the Governor's daughter takes ill, and we learn in a flashback that the young man is the son of the Lord of Pavonia (New Jersey), who saved her from an attack by an Indian as she walked in the woods on his side of the river. The fathers of the couple have been bitterly feuding over fishing rights to the river, and when Blandina reveals to her father two days before the scheduled execution that the man is her husband, the Governor, outraged, says she is no longer his daughter and that the man will hang along with the dominie who married them. Just before the execution is to take place, however, the Lord of Pavonia crosses over to New Amsterdam and offers to surrender the right of the river to the high water mark in exchange for the life of his son. The Governor and his council accept the offer, and in time the two families become united. The wife of Aurie, we learn, is the granddaughter of the young couple in the story, and Jan Sol, we also learn, insisted to his dying day that the young Lord of Pavonia and the specter were two different persons.

Although "The Little Dutch Sentinel" is a ghost story, it contains nothing truly supernatural. On the contrary, Paulding's intimate knowledge of old Dutch customs and attitudes allows him to present a realistic rendering of New Amsterdam life. Moreover, while the story entertains through humor and suspense, it also develops the theme of the admirable frankness, sturdiness, and simplicity of the colonists. Surrounded by things they do not understand, such as the Indians and witchcraft, they manfully struggle to define and comprehend the New World.

Jan Sol obviously represents the weaker side of the community whose failure to perceive clearly gives credence to superstitions and thus disrupts the social order. On the other hand, the Governor and his council, severe though they are, represent the rational and skeptical cast of mind necessary for the survival of all. Even the apparently subversive young Lord of Pavonia frankly acknowledges his guilt and stoically accepts his sentence. Because the ideals of certainty and order lie at the heart of the work, the resolution of the dispute over the river boundary serves as a well-chosen conclusion to the story.

"Cobus Yerks"

"Cobus Yerks" (1828), like "The Little Dutch Sentinel," is a humorous, well-told ghost story about the New York Dutch. Resembling "The Legend of Sleepy Hollow" in its structure, it lacks the mellow charm of Irving's story yet possesses a more realistic and sympathetic portrayal of character. It takes place on a Tuesday in November 1793, the day on which the unnamed narrator was poisoned by a dish of Souchong tea. As he lies ill, Cobus Yerkes, a superstitious Dutch farmer who lives in a remote spot on the Sawmill River, travels into the little market town on the Hudson. While there, Cobus looks into the village inn, "just to say How d'ye to the landlady"[4] and finds everyone discussing the poisoning, which by then had been extended to the whole family, "not one of whom had been left alive by the bloody-minded damsel, Rumour" (79).

As Cobus listens horrorstruck, one Timothy Canty, a bug collector and sleigh painter whom Paulding describes at length, arrives. Tim, "the merriest rogue in the world, even when the fog was at the thickest" (75), says he has learned that not only has the whole family died, but all the animals as well, except for a black bulldog, who came to life and ran away howling like a devil incarnate. Tim has seen where the dog jumped over the barnyard gate, he says, "and there was the print of a cloven foot, as plain as the daylight this blessed minute" (81).

The sun has already set, of course, and as Tim proceeds to tell more stories, each more appalling than the first, Cobus, "a true disciple of the doctrine that spirit and courage, that is to say, whiskey and valour were synonomous" (82), drinks from his jug and huddles in the chimney corner. As the evening wears on and everyone leaves, Cobus stays put. "Gradually all became quiet within and without the house," Paulding writes, "except now and then the howling of a wandering cur, and the still more doleful moaning of the winds, accompanied by the hollow thumping of the waves, as they dashed on the rock shores of the river than ran hard by" (82). Finally, at the landlady's insistence, Cobus unsteadily leaves, but he never arrives home.

The following morning a search party, formed by his wife, looks for him, and they find his broadbrimmed hat on the road, then the backboard of his wagon, then a shoe, and finally the fragments of his wagon with his horses standing quietly close by. After looking around, they find Cobus, lying apparently dead among the briars. When they hold his jug under his nose, however, his eyes open, his lips smack, and he exclaims, "Some o' that boys" (85). After being taken to the tavern, he tells his tale.

He says he started rather late from the town, having been "kept there—by business" (86), and as he passed the spot where the killer John Ryder was hung, he heard "somebody coming, pat, pat, pat, close behind" his wagon. The sound of the steps became louder and louder, and when he looked back, he saw a pair of saucer eyes "as big and as bright as the mouths of a fiery furnace" (87). Taking "another little dram," he made the whip fly about the ears of his horses; then he heard something heavy jump into the wagon with a "bang!" Looking over his shoulder, he saw "great burning eyes" within a half a yard of his back and smelled the breath of the creature, which was "exactly like brimstone" (87). As his horses went faster and faster, Cobus relates, he came to the bridge at old Mangham's, where a black shaggy dog jumped onto the front seat and, snatching the whip and reins and whispering something in Cobus's ear, the dog lashed away on the horses "till they seemed to fly through the air" (87). Finally, the smell of brimstone became overpowering, Cobus says, and that was the last he could remember.

This story is doubted by some who hint that the burning eyes and brimstone breath belonged to Cobus's great housedog that had followed him that day to the village and was found quietly resting by his master. Cobus, however, thereafter knocked anyone down who asserted "that the contents of the stone jug were at the bottom of the whole business" (88), and his story became incorporated into the marvelous legends of the area.

As should be clear from the above summary, Paulding's story is fast paced, well plotted, humorous, and rich in local color. The character of Tim Canty, based apparently upon one of Paulding's childhood friends, is well developed, and the setting, profiting from Paulding's knowledge of the Tarrytown region, is also described with accuracy. In fact, he captures well the spirit of the small town and the attitudes of the inhabitants; the tavern, the talk, the countryside, the sights and sounds of the night all are described with a concreteness that makes the scene come alive. Perhaps more importantly, the story reveals a keen insight into human nature, particularly Cobus's frailty, and successfully draws from it good-natured humor that has retained its freshness over the years.

"The Dumb Girl"

Of only slightly less merit than Paulding's best two Dutch stories is "The Dumb Girl" (1829), a moving tale of sin and guilt that apparently influenced Hawthorne's writing of *The Scarlet Letter.*[5] The story, autobiographical in origin, opens with the narrator relating that twenty years before there lived on a corner of his uncle's farm an impoverished family named Angevine. The father is a loafer, the mother a fool, the son an idiot, and the daughter, Phoebe, a beautiful, industrious mute girl of sixteen, whose only faults are a streak of vanity about her appearance and a passionate nature inculcated by the reading of fashionable novels.

After reaching the flirtatious age of eighteen, Phoebe attracts the attentions of Walter Avery, the handsome, callous son of a rich neighboring squire. As the local gossips wag their tongues in disapproval, Walter, with no intentions of marrying Phoebe, uses expensive gifts and walks in the woods to seduce her. As Paulding explains, "In the wicked twilight of the quiet woods the purest heart sometimes swells with the boiling eddies of a youthful fancy; and it is there that the purest person is won to the permission of little freedoms and progressive endearments, which, if not checked in time, are only atoned for by the tears of a whole life."[6] Predictably, one day Phoebe becomes pregnant, and after a meeting with Walter, disappears. Circumstantial evidence suggests that she was murdered at his hands.

Although insufficient evidence exists for Walter's arrest, the judgment of society and the torment of his conscience make his life miserable. As years pass, he becomes misanthropic, eventually marrying a shrew, who dies several years later. Subsequently, he dreams about Phoebe, and one evening a young boy appears before him with a note from her, revealing that the boy is their son and that she still lives. We learn that at their last meeting she had thrown herself in the river in despair and he had failed to see her climb out downstream. After living for seven years in a distant township, she heard of his plight and has returned to the area temporarily to give their son to him to raise, which he subsequently does. When the boy reaches manhood, Walter takes sick, and Phoebe goes to him. In a touching death-bed scene, he asks her forgiveness and receives it. They are then married by a local clergyman two weeks before Walter's death, and, as a rich widow, Phoebe in time becomes an admired member of the community.

Although "The Dumb Girl" has been cited by some Paulding scholars as his best short work, it lacks the firm sense of place and fidelity to life of the two Dutch tales discussed above. Moreover, Paulding's two main characters resemble too closely the stock villain and heroine of the sentimental novel, even though one theme of the work is the dangers of such fiction. To its credit, however, the story is tightly structured, thoughtful, and touching. It is also ahead of its time in its exploration of the psychological effects of guilt, with Walter's deterioration being convincingly portrayed. As noted above, several critics believe that *The Scarlet Letter* is indebted to the story, and the strongest piece of evidence is the following entry that appeared in Hawthorne's *American Notebooks* for September 7, 1835: "A young man to win the love of a girl, without any serious intentions, and to find that in that love, which might have been the greatest blessing of his life, he had conjured up a spirit of mischief which pursued him throughout his whole career——and this without any revengeful purposes on the part of the deserted girl."[7] A number of parallels between the story and the novel, which grew out of this entry, can be seen, but ultimately, of course, Paulding's modest achievement pales in comparison to Hawthorne's rich masterpiece. To the first should indeed go the credit due innovation, but to the second that due mastery.

"Childe Roeliff's Pilgrimage"

Although ignored by Paulding scholars, "Childe Roeliff's Pilgrimage; A Travelling Legend," published in *Tales of Glauber-Spa*

(1832), ranks high among his best fiction. Set in the summer of 1828, it is an entertaining contemporary love story, filled with biting social satire and well-drawn sketches of American scenery. Its rather conventional plot focuses upon a forthright and poor young gentleman named Reuben Rossmore, who vies with an unscrupulous, refined dandy named Julius Dibdill for the hand of Minerva Orendorf, a beautiful, intelligent, but immature girl of eighteen. During the course of a family pleasure trip from New York City to Montreal, with stops at Albany, a pioneer home in the wilderness, Saratoga Springs, and Lake George, Minerva overcomes her infatuation with Dibdill and falls in love with Reuben.

The characters begin as types, but through extensive use of dialogue, much of it witty, Paulding endows them with creditable roundness and believability. Also, his detailed descriptions of the social world of the Springs and of the scenery around Lake George give the story a forceful sense of place that serves to define the characters. The denouement wherein Minerva's proud, pragmatic father, Roeliff, overhears a conversation about himself between the idealistic Reuben and the cynical Dibdill is particularly moving, and the exchanges among the three, while obviously contrived for the purposes of climax, are well prepared for by all that has gone before. Apart from its hackneyed plot, the main weakness of the story, some eighty pages in length, is its lack of compression caused by Paulding's digressions upon the scenery, the manners, and the modes of behavior of the time. For the student of social history, however, these digressions add to the story's appeal.

"The Adventures of Henry Bird"

"The Adventures of Henry Bird" (*Analectic Magazine*, October 1815) is a gripping narrative that anticipated Cooper's use of frontier characters and frontier lore by some eight years.[8] The story is an account of Bird's Indian captivity apparently drawn from a personal interview Paulding conducted with the man in the summer of 1815. In 1797 Bird settled at the headwaters of the Sandusky, in the state of Ohio. The Indians were at first friendly, but on October 17, 1811, after the battle of Tippecanoe, a band of eighteen Shawnee attacked the settlers, killing Bird's wife and five children and brutally hacking his side and shoulder with tomahawks. Taken captive, he was forced to journey with the Indians some four hundred miles to their camp, there becoming a white slave.

Suspected of plotting escape, Bird had his two thumbnails twisted off, and in February 1815, after escaping and being recaptured, he was tied to the ground on his back and tortured with fire brands for three days at half-hour intervals. Paulding writes, "the fingers of his right hand were almost consumed, and his arm burnt quite to the bone. I saw his hand and arm myself, or I could never have been brought to believe that human nature could have endured such long suffering."[9]

Bird was finally ransomed by a Scotch trader from Quebec named Randall M'Donald, and after being cared for by M'Donald, he eventually made his way to Washington to seek aid for the white women still held captive, arriving July 6, 1815. In his conclusion, Paulding pays tribute to Bird by reporting, "there was a striking manliness in his deportment, and he told his tale with such an air of simple truth, that I could swear to every word of it. I asked if he had any objection to its being made public? He said none, provided I did not make a fine story about him" (36).

Although journalistic in style, the story is one of Paulding's most powerful works, with much of its power arising from his direct, understated treatment of his material. True to his word, he did not embellish Bird's account, but, as W. T. Conklin has pointed out, "the attention to detail and the emphasis upon pioneer character display a conscious artistry."[10] Much like modern writers such as Truman Capote and Norman Mailer, Paulding successfully creates an intense realism here by journalistically drawing his material from actual events and then invisibly but artistically shaping these materials into a dramatic construct.

In addition to the five stories discussed above, Paulding wrote three others of literary merit, "The Mother's Tragedy," "Poor Genevieve," and "The White Indian," but neither they, nor others praised by Paulding scholars, deserve discussion here. The extent of Paulding's success in the short-story genre was limited, and unless this is acknowledged, an inaccurate estimate of his achievement emerges. Amos L. Herold has called the years 1824 to 1832 "the Paulding decade of the short story" because "he averaged five or six stories annually, and published them either in the leading periodicals or in book form";[11] however, unless one is particularly impressed by quantity, Paulding's productivity should reflect little credit upon him. In fact, as Herold himself suggests, one wishes Paulding had written less and written better.

Nevertheless, at a time when the short story had not yet been recognized as a legitimate literary genre, at a time, in fact, when few knew how to construct unified, compressed, and meaningful shorter pieces of fiction, Paulding did better than most. At least two of his tales would certainly not suffer in comparison with others in an anthology of American literature and would indeed stand out in an anthology of nineteenth-century local-color writing. Furthermore, taken as a whole, the five stories discussed in this chapter constitute a respectable contribution to a native American literature and indicate that Paulding came close to being Irving's equal in the development of the American short story.

Chapter Eight

Novels

As a novelist, Paulding struggled to reconcile his critical preference for literary realism with his readers' thirst for supernatural horrors, false sentiments, idealized characters, and romantic adventures. Because he wished to be read, his choices were to write Gothic novels, sentimental novels, or historical romances, all best sellers of the day, but none of which, as defined by the practice of others, met his standard of naturalness. Compaining all the while, he chose to write historical romances, five of them, doing his best at first to challenge the conventions of the genre and eventually to reshape it in accordance with his critical theories, which insisted upon originality, nationality, and wholesomeness in addition to naturalness. In the process he produced two excellent novels and one good one.

The latter was his first, *Koningsmarke* (1823), which, although marred by uncertainty of purpose and carelessness of execution, is distinguished by its innovative and amusing satire. In it Paulding tried to writc an ingratiating historical romancc whilc maintaining and displaying a disdain for the genre—an impossible task. During the eight years before he published his second novel, he wrote more than a dozen short stories and his play *The Lion of the West*, efforts that apparently taught him to treat his own fiction with more respect and to dramatize his material with more skill. *The Dutchman's Fireside* (1831) and *Westward Ho!* (1832), both of which deal with American materials and themes, can stand comparison with the best works of Cooper and Simms. In them, Paulding's abilities as story teller, local colorist, satirist, social critic, and dramatist provide a zesty salmagundi brew that has retained its flavor over the years. Both novels have complex structures in which characters and themes are developed with care; also, they contain a fast-paced combination of dialogue and action, which engages and holds the reader's attention. When Paulding wrote his last two novels, *The Old Continental* (1846) and *The Puritan and His Daughter* (1849), he was in his late sixties and had not published a novel in some fifteen years. Predictably, his age and rustiness show, and both works can be dismissed with brief attention here, before we turn to the three better novels that preceded them.

The Old Continental

The Old Continental; or, The Price of Liberty focuses on the Revolutionary War adventures of a poor, nineteen-year-old farm boy named John, whose home is in the Neutral Ground between New York City (occupied by the British) and the Hudson Highlands (controlled by the Continental Army). According to Paulding's Preface, he wished to convey "some idea of the spirit, the sufferings, and the sacrifices of a class of people who are seldom, if ever, individualized in history, yet who always bear the brunt of war and invasion." Paulding obviously had his own family in mind, and his hero's adventures are based on those of his cousin John Paulding.

As several critics have pointed out, the novel gives a more authentic account of the Neutral Ground than does Cooper's *The Spy* (1821), set in the same place and time. Because Paulding grew up in Westchester County, he possessed intimate knowledge of its scenery and the sufferings and hardships its inhabitants had to endure during the war. As a result, the strength of the novel is its vivid and convincing descriptions of the rural countryside, of the plight of the American troops wintering in the Highlands, and of the miserable conditions on the British prison ships in New York City, where John and his father were confined.

Unfortunately, Paulding's characters lack the credibility of his settings. Because of the awe with which he regarded his tall, strong, daring cousin, some twenty years his senior, and because (as discussed in Chapter 1) he wished to counter the aspersions cast upon John in 1817, Paulding made his hero out to be so patriotic, so dedicated to his country and to the task of earning honor, that he bears little resemblance to a real life figure. John's speeches consistently display an overblown rhetoric, reminiscent of a bad stage play, written by sixth graders, for a patriotic occasion. Also, John's adventures generate little natural suspense, for he steadily travels the road to glory and matrimony by handily overcoming the series of challenges to his life and honor.

Most disappointing of all, the climax of the narrative, the capture of André, falls flat. In the events leading up to the capture, Paulding dissipates the energy of his work by shifting the point of view back and forth between André and John, failing to see that while this might satisfy readers fascinated by the handsome young spy, it detracts from the sympathy and stature he has spent pages trying to give to his own protagonist. Although Paulding insists that John and his fellows deserve more respect than André, he allows them to be diminished by him. In short then, *The Old Continental* could have been one of Paulding's best works, given the inherently engaging materials he was dealing with and his inside information about them; however, it is not.

The Puritan and His Daughter

Although *The Puritan and His Daughter* is the weakest of Paulding's novels, it possesses a strong plot, at least for an historical romance. It opens in England in 1645 when tensions between Puritans and the Crown were reaching the breaking point. Harold Habingdon, a young aristocrat, falls in love with Susan Baneswright, a devout young Puritan, and after becoming a convert to her faith, he fights with Cromwell's army, marrying her at the end of the war and settling on his family estate.

When the Royalists return to power, the Puritan and his family journey to the New World to escape persecution, arriving in Virginia where they settle near Hugh Tyringham, a loyal Cavalier. The Puritan's daughter, Miriam, and Tyringham's son, Langley, fall in love, but their parents forbid them to see one another. An Indian raid brings the two families together briefly, but the Habingtons then move to New England where they face another Indian raid. Miriam's parents eventually die; she is accused of witchcraft, saved from execution at the last minute, and reunited with Langley, who, while searching for her, has endured shipwreck and Indian captivity. As the novel ends, the lovers begin their return to the Tyringham estate in Virginia.

Interwoven into this plot is an engaging theme: the healthy resistance to bigotry and persecution to be found in parts of the New World; however, Paulding's overall treatment of his materials is uninspired. In a letter to a friend, he thus described his efforts to satisfy his publishers, Baker and Scribner: "Having nothing to do in the Farming way this winter, I have undertaken to *Splice* the Puritans Daughter, as they do Steam Boats, by cutting them in two, and putting a piece in the middle. With dovetailing here a little, and there a little—loitering by the way, and stopping now and then to have a talk—like Cooper, I shall be able to stretch it to the proper dimensions, I hope, without doing it much damage" (*Letters*, 490–91). Not surprisingly, the novel in its final form is rambling and dull. In addition, its settings, particularly those in England (where Paulding had never been), are vague, and its characters are all wooden.

Koningsmarke

Of greater literary merit than his last two novels, Paulding's first, *Koningsmarke, The Long Finne, A Story of the New World* (1823), is a high-spirited work he obviously took much pleasure writing and no pains polishing. He explained to his friend Irving that it "was written for no earthly purpose but to pass the leisure hours of about six weeks that I was left alone at Washington, Gertrude and the children being on a visit to New York" (*Letters*, 68–69). The recent and startling success of Cooper as a rival to Scott probably also influenced his decision to try this new genre. He half-jokingly admits as much in the novel, declaring, "to confess the honest truth, we are . . . rather new in the trade of novel writing, having been partly induced to enter upon it, as people engage in the tobacco or grocery line, from seeing others prosper mightily in the business."[1]

The unusual distinguishing feature of this historical romance is its seriocomic tone, and Paulding's decision to imitate Fielding's practice in *Tom Jones* of introducing each book with a discursive introductory chapter accounts in part for this. The novel is divided into nine books, and in the nine introductory essays, Paulding offers various satirical observations on the writing of historical romances. Scattered throughout the narrative are additional satirical elements that further mock the adventure story itself. For example, his main character, Koningsmarke, at times becomes a parody of the gloomy Byronic hero haunted by mysterious guilt; a minor character, "Bombie of the Frizzled Head," an old domestic slave, is a take-off of Scott's "Norna of the Fitful Head," who appears in *The Pirate* (1822); and the torture scenes are so excessively detailed and bloody that they seem partially intended to parody the horrors of the Gothic novel. Similarly, Paulding uses the character Wolfgang Langfanger, an advocate of internal improvements, to ridicule the doctrines of Henry Clay, and the character Dominie Kanttwell, a greedy, hypocritical minister, to poke fun at religious fanaticism and misplaced philanthropy. Moving among these satirical elements, though not too comfortably, is the narrative itself, consisting of a series of adventures held loosely together by a love interest that becomes slightly wearisome in its prolongation.

The novel is set in the town of Elsingburgh, a Swedish possession in the New World, governed by the testy Heer Peter Piper, father of the beautiful, sweet heroine, Christina. The time is about the middle of the seventeenth century (when the English, not the Swedes, were in control, as Paulding well knew), and on the scene arrives a tall, blue-eyed youth called Koningsmarke, claiming to be the nephew of one of Piper's boyhood friends. The youth has been arrested for possessing a handful of English coins, and Piper, irritated by the young man's defiant manner, has him imprisoned without food, but Christina, smitten from a distance by his looks, sends him nightly suppers by way of the family servant, Bombie. Soon the jail catches fire, and the injured youth is taken into Piper's house, where he is nursed back to health by Christina. The two fall in love, of course, although Bombie warns her mistress not to trust him. He subsequently saves Christina from the attack of a mad hermit in the woods, and in the process discloses a scar on his neck that horrifies her by evoking a vague childhood memory. As the two prepare to marry, a neighboring tribe of Indians, enraged by Piper's damming of their river and Dominie Kanttwell's efforts to convert them, attack the settlement and take Koningsmarke, Christina, and several others captive. The Indians gruesomely torture and murder two captives, but the young lovers' lives are spared when an Indian widow takes Koningsmarke as her slave and an Indian girl, named Deer Eyes, adopts Christina as her sister.

After Koningsmarke heroically battles along side of his captors against an Indian tribe in Ohio, his Indian owner decides to marry him. To prevent this, Koningsmarke and Christina escape, only to be recaptured and brought back to the camp, where Koningsmarke is sentenced to die by torture. Deer Eyes, who has fallen in love with him, secures him a brief reprieve by interpreting a thunderclap as the voice of the angry Spirit, and before the delayed torture begins, he and Christina are ransomed by a band of Quakers sent by William Penn.

After their return to the settlement, the English arrive and demand the surrender of Elsingburgh, and as Piper is complying, Koningsmarke mysteriously disappears. Several weeks later, Piper and Christina learn that he is a prisoner of the British in New York City, convicted of conspiring with the Indians, and that he has been condemned to be sold into slavery in the Barbadoes. After traveling to New York, they successfully plead his case with Governor Lovelace, who suggests that the couple be married in his city. At this point Koningsmarke reveals to Christina that he was present when a band of outlaws killed her mother, but that he was their captive at the time. All is forgiven, the marriage takes place, and they retire to a beautiful farm on the banks of a little river, soon adding a blue-eyed son to the family.

When Paulding's first novel appeared, only a few American periodicals gave it much notice, and their responses were mixed and confused. The reviewer for the *Minerva*, after pointing out that the novel's jests were trite, its incidents hackneyed, and its style careless, curiously called it "a valuable acquisition to our national literature" and praised "the genius, talent, and spirit displayed" in it.[2] Similarly, the reviewer for the *New-York Mirror* chided the anonymous author for his careless grammar and attacks on Scott but declared that "the incident . . . is natural and deeply interesting; the style is in general smooth, classical and frequently sublime."[3]

Response to the novel in England was more abundant, but similarly inconsistent. The *Literary Gazette* found it "sometimes inclined to coarseness, and not always polished in style," but "altogether the most amusing novel which has crossed the Atlantic." The *Literary Examiner* judged it inferior to Cooper's novels but conceded that "it exhibits an occasional power of description, and still more, a considerable portion of light and easy humour, which makes it bearable and even entertaining." A bit more positively, the *British Magazine, or Miscellany of Polite Literature*, while criticizing Paulding's "excessive fondness for the ludicrous," found him "upon the whole, very amusing" and his work "an important addition to the small stock of American literature."[4]

Modern critical opinion of *Koningsmarke* has proved both more positive and more negative than that of the contemporary reviews. On the positive side, Vernon L. Parrington has called it "Paulding's most interesting book," adding that "it is native and original, full of shrewd comment and sly satire. . . . Few books of the time are more amusing." Albert Keiser has agreed that it is "one of the finest" of Paulding's works "composed in his lighter vein," and he has declared that the account of Koningsmarke's combat with the Ohio Indians "hardly ever has been excelled in the description of battle scenes anywhere." Alexander Cowie, while objecting to Paulding's bantering tone, has also praised the adventure story, which "goes through phases that are so thrilling or chilling as one may care to read." Finally, in the highest estimate yet offered, Harold E. Hall has called it "probably the most interesting and most significant of all [Paulding's] longer works in fiction."[5]

On the negative side, Amos L. Herold, while crediting the work with realistic characters and a "finely conceived and convincingly written" thunder scene, has seen in it "the marks of an initial, imitative effort." "It is," Herold writes, "deficient in unity and cumulative force." James Holman Robertson has also judged it as deeply flawed due to inconsistencies in Paulding's characterizations, and, Thomas F. O'Donnell, in the most astute analysis of the novel yet published, has argued that in spite of its merits, the novel fails in its grand purpose. He points out that Paulding began by writing a satire of the historical romance yet apparently changed his mind during the writing. "The blatantly contrived denouement has the ring of spoof, to be sure," O'Donnell writes, "but Paulding here recalls his promise and original intention only after many chapters in which the satire, if there is any at all, is almost unrecognizable. From about the middle of Book II on, *Koningsmarke* becomes, not an attack on, but another example of extravagant romance."[6]

Ultimately, the uncertainy of purpose in *Koningsmarke* makes it fall slightly short of excellence. If viewed as a historical romance, it appears shabbily outfitted in some of the most threadbare conventions of that genre. We have the protracted love affair, the death-defying feats of bravery, the mystery, the hairbreadth escapes, but little sense of place, little thematic richness. Because Paulding obviously had little respect for the historical romance as a genre, he felt free to write without concentration or seriousness. This also shows in his self-revealing remarks about inconsistencies in characterization, improbabilities in plot, padding, and a variety of other satiric irregularities. Near the end, in fact, when he explains the mystery surrounding Koningsmarke's past and Christina's childhood memory, he admits that the reader has been intentionally misled about the truth of his hero's character. Although such tomfoolery may allow the novel to escape the demands placed upon more serious historical romances, and although it does generate eccentric humor, the attitude of author toward reader it implies is disturbing.

The fact that Paulding's disdain for his story ultimately extends to disdain for the reader as well is the novel's major flaw. As previously mentioned, the introductory chapters are modeled on those found in Fielding's *Tom Jones*, but while the digressions of the two authors deal with similar topics such as the prevailing taste for romances, the importance of drawing from nature, and the scurrilousness of critics, their effects are quite different. In his essays, Fielding shows himself to be aware of his reader's thoughts and feelings and strives to present himself as an interested acquaintance (a fellow traveler, on a stage, as he says); Paulding, however, makes little attempt to be sociable and, in fact, begins by speaking ironically and adopting the pose of a writer of romances, who, because the conventions allow it, will be as inconsistent and unrealistic in his narrative as he pleases. Fielding, as he describes the requisites for a great writer or teases his reader about Tom's possible fate, exhibits a consistent goodwill; Paulding, however, while ironic to begin with, becomes carping as he attacks the conventions of the historical romance, and finally insulting as he discusses his prolixity that is required to fill two volumes. Ultimately, Fielding most successfully gains the reader's goodwill by insisting that the work he is writing is true to nature. Thus, when he attacks the use of the marvellous and defines the great writer as one who studies nature and portrays it, the reader, because he is being offered something of worth, perceives and appreciates Fielding's respect. Paulding, however, implies that his book is being written to please the popular taste and is thus inherently worthless. Consequently, if the reader is caught up in the narrative or finds it enjoyable, he finally has to deal with the discomforting knowledge that Paulding views him as a fool.

The Dutchman's Fireside

Fortunately, in his second novel, *The Dutchman's Fireside*, Paulding abandoned the mockery of *Koningsmarke* and carefully, with no sense of uncertainty or shame, wrote a historical romance that is one of the finest of its day. Although the work contains much silly dialogue, several embarrassingly stock scenes, and some jarring racist and sexist humor, its plot is superbly constructed, its characters engaging and real, its descriptions rich in local color, and its themes original and profound.

The convincing rendering of the novel's main character, Sybrant Westbrook, owes much to the autobiographical traits Paulding gives him. As the novel opens "somewhere about the time of the old French War"[7] (the late 1750s), Sybrant is a handsome, intelligent, and learned young Dutchman, who is also introverted, rustic, and ungainly. He lives with his stepfather, Dennis Vancour, on a Hudson estate some one hundred miles from Albany, and the plot of the novel, which has a symmetry and unity unusual in Paulding's works, concerns Sybrant's struggles to achieve manhood and win the hand of his beloved cousin, Catalina. Scenes at the rural Vancour estate, where Catalina also lives, frame the novel, and within this frame, the journeys Sybrant takes and the foes he encounters are carefully selected to portray his development into an experienced and graceful adult.

In the opening scenes, Sybrant suffers from shyness and fright whenever Catalina is near, and she in turn, though fond of him, takes pleasure in teasing him and then becomes affronted by his proud responses. Their romance prospers slightly when, during a group picnic on an island in the Hudson, a flash flood occurs and he saves her from drowning. It soon suffers a setback, however, when British troops arrive in the area and Catalina coquettishly flirts with a decadent Colonel Sydenham, favored by her class-conscious mother.

Upset by Catalina's behavior, Sybrant goes on a trading voyage into the wilderness. Very much a rite of passage, the voyage eventually gives him experiential knowledge to complement that he has gained through the study of books. With his black servant, "the dusky Charon, old Tjerck," he travels toward the sources of the Hudson and the heart of the American wilderness until they encounter a band of Mohawks, whose demoniacal one-eyed leader, Paskingoe, proposes to take them to tribesmen having beaver skins to trade. As they travel deeper into the wilderness, Sybrant's and Tjerck's suspicions mount regarding the intent of the savages, and Paulding's descriptions skillfully reflect the hellish nature of their situation. Paddling "along the devious windings of the lazy solitary stream, that seemed a vast serpent asleep in the high grass that skirted its banks," they feel "lost in the pathless monotony of the vast meadows" and hear amid the silence only the dipping of the paddles, "like the clicking of the death-watch when all else is still" (1:90). That night as a storm rages outside their shelter, Paskingoe and his followers, in drunken fury, attack Sybrant, who kills Paskingoe and is about to be killed himself by the rest when Sir William Johnson, Indian agent to the Six Nations, bursts upon the scene and saves his life.

As Sybrant recovers from wounds sustained in the fray, Sir William cares for him at his woodland village and protects him from the Mohawks who seek his life. During the course of a fall and winter, Sir William, in contrast to Sybrant's boyhood tutor, Dominie Stettinius, teaches the youth the primacy of action to thought, and through the activities of hunting and fishing, Sybrant gradually forsakes his melancholy meditative habits and acquires new confidence in himself.

Upon returning home, Sybrant impresses Catalina with a new grace and ease of manner, but he still finds it awkward to be in her presence. Although the British have left the scene, a new antagonist appears, Hans Pipe, a semicivilized savage, who is given to drink and violence. When Sybrant fights and defeats Pipe during one of his drunken rampages, the savage swears vengeance and secretly plots to murder Catalina. After various complications, Sybrant saves her life and kills Pipe after a hand-to-hand combat on the edge of a cliff. In a subsequent romantic scene, the young couple pledge their love to one another, but Madame Vancour interrupts their courtship by sending Catalina to New York City for a long visit.

The opening scenes of the novel's second volume focus on Catalina's journey south on the Hudson and her successes in the fashionable world of New York City. Her hostess, Mrs. Aubineau, schemes to marry the girl to a British officer and prefers the first of two suitors, Sir Thickness Throgmorton and Barry Gilfillan, because of his title. Paulding has great fun detailing Throgmorton's dull stupidity and

Gilfillan's charming hypocrisy, but eventually he brings Sybrant back on the scene through an invitation to him from Mr. Aubineau, who thinks the youth is being ill used.

The rural young Dutchman cuts a poor figure in the fashionable world of New York, however, and his snuff-colored breeches, years out of date, make him the laughing stock of the Governor's Ball which he attends. Catalina is briefly ashamed of her fiancé, and when Sybrant senses this, he withdraws from the scene, but not before warning Gilfillan to abandon his suit. Taking the youth for a bumpkin, Gilfillan responds with an insult, but to his surprise, Sybrant coolly challenges him to a duel. Before the two can meet at dawn of the next day, Gilfillan is sent to the frontier to fight against the French and the Indians, but prior to his departure, he kisses Catalina goodbye, against her will, and Sybrant, arriving on the scene unannounced, misinterprets the relationship between the two and silently departs.

After meeting with Sir William at the Vancour estate, Sybrant goes with him on a second trip to the wilderness, this time to fight as a volunteer in the war. At Fort Ticonderoga he distinguishes himself as a fine soldier, and consequently Sir William sends him and Timothy Weasel, an Indian hater and fighter, on a spying mission in the dead of night into the enemy's camp to learn their number and intentions. When the dangerous mission succeeds, Sybrant Westbrook is made Major Westbrook.

Based on the information gained by his spies, Sir William advises General Abercrombie, the British officer in charge of the fort, to keep his troops within, but Abercrombie instead marches his men out into the forest to confront the enemy. They are ambushed, and only the bravery of Sir William, Sybrant, the other provincials, and and their Mohawk allies saves the British from total defeat. Wounded in the battle, Sybrant recovers in the same room as Gilfillan, whose life he has saved in battle and who now lies dying. Before his death, Gilfillan explains to Sybrant that Catalina has remained true to him and still loves him. His spirits lifted, Sybrant writes to Catalina and her father, but a half-breed messenger loses the letters in route and returns to tell him that his letters were laughed at and received no replies. As Sybrant struggles to deal with this misinformation, the Vancours learn that he has died. When he finally returns home, he is mistaken for a ghost, but the various misunderstandings are quickly cleared up, and he is reunited with Catalina. At the wedding supper, Sir William, who regards Sybrant now as a son, is in attendance, reminding him of the importance of action.

The well-constructed plot of *The Dutchman's Fireside*, as well as the major characters and dramatic events, are all of Paulding's creation; however, several settings, some minor characters, and much of the local color concerning old Dutch life are indebted to *The Memoirs of An American Lady* (1808) by Mrs. Anne Grant. In the Advertisement at the front of his novel, Paulding acknowledges that "the idea of the following tale was conceived on reading, many years ago," Mrs. Grant's *Memoirs*, "one of the finest sketches of early American manners ever drawn." Mrs. Grant, formerly Anne MacVicar, was the daughter of a captain in a Scottish regiment stationed near Albany from 1758 to 1768. Although she wrote her *Memoirs* some forty years after leaving America at the age of thirteen, she successfully recalled the manners, customs, and natural surroundings she observed as a child. Some of the particular materials Paulding borrowed from her for his own work include the tradition of a trading voyage undertaken by Dutch youths to prove themselves worthy of their brides; the picnic on an island in the Hudson; the three Dutch brothers living near each other on an estate near Albany; the secret contempt by British officers for the Dutch settlers; the Dominie's unsuccessful battle against the adoption by Dutch youths of the dress and manners of the British; the description of Sir William Johnson, including his conduct, his village, his Indian wife, and his dealings with the Indians; and finally, the unfavorable portrait of General Abercrombie and his disastrous methods of waging war in the wilderness.[8]

James Fenimore Cooper, in his novel *Satanstoe* (1845), often compared with *The Dutchman's Fireside*, also borrowed, with acknowledgment, from Mrs. Grant, and Paulding's example probably inspired him to do so. Cooper thought highly of Paulding's work in general and *The Dutchman's Fireside* in particular. In a letter of June 1831, he placed Paulding among "men of genius," as opposed to "small, namby pamby writers," and in November of that year, he wrote from Paris to his publishers asking "Did you publish Paulding's book?" (They did not.) "I have just read it," he goes on, "and I think it quite good—Some parts excellent, but very unequal. . . . It is the only American novel I have read since I left home [1826], and

I must say I think the species improves." After criticizing Paulding's portrait of Sir William Johnson, which he thought little resembled the actual man, Cooper adds, "But the book has capital things in it."[9]

Contemporary readers of the novel appear to have agreed with Cooper. James D. Hart lists it as the one book most widely read in America in the years immediately following its publication in 1831, and, according to Amos L. Herold, by 1852 it had gone through seven editions in America, four in England, and had been translated into French (1832), Swedish (1833), German (1837 and 1838), Dutch (1838), and Danish (1838).[10] Reviewers of the book in America were generally pleased with it also. Although the *New England Magazine* and the *New-York Mirror* both criticized Paulding's stylistic lapses, the latter went on to declare that he "seems not inferior, in the extent and diversity of his talents, to any American writer of the present school," and it praised the novel's "keen insight into the human character," its "deep and striking observations," its "racy original humor," and its "total absence of display or affectation."[11]

Cooper had predicted that the book would fare poorly in England "for it hits John too hard (not for the truth) but for that gentleman's taste,"[12] and he proved mostly right. While the British reviewers praised Paulding's vigorous descriptions, engaging incidents, and accurate local color, they too objected to his "often inelegant and florid" style[13] and his bias against the British. The *Westminster Review*, however, presented a minority view by applauding Paulding's "chaste and elegant" style and finding him "neither too elaborate like Irving, nor diffuse like Cooper, nor 'wild, and all but frantic, like Neal," but instead "just, neat, fanciful, and descriptive."[14]

During the twentieth century *The Dutchman's Fireside* has been generally regarded as Paulding's best novel, at least by those who have read his works, and although its flaws have been duly pointed out, a variety of its features have received attention and praise. Amos L. Herold, Vernon L. Parrington, and Thomas F. O'Donnell have emphasized its authentic and pleasurable account of the New York Dutch before the Revolution.[15] Arthur Hobson Quinn has praised the "vivid description of the defeat of Abercrombie before Ticonderoga"; James Holman Robertson has lauded Paulding's descriptions of Hudson River Valley scenery and his penetrating psychological analysis of Sybrant; and Floyd C. Watkins has singled out the scene where Weasel and Sybrant confront the Indians, declaring, "For pure adventure and action this incident is perhaps not surpassed in any American story of frontier life."[16] Finally, in a superb recent study of the novel, Leland S. Person, Jr., has detailed how it "stands out as a rarity among nineteenth-century romances" by its presentation of "an alternative myth of the wilderness—a fable of initiation whose goal is a compromise between the too often exclusive claims for the wilderness and civilization."[17]

As these comments indicate, *The Dutchman's Fireside* is a vital, able-bodied creation, and its musculature becomes even more impressive when examined closely. Although the novel does delineate what Cowie has called the "mild thesis" that "a life of action is the cure for one who suffers from the mental or psychological ills of civilization,"[18] this idea is only one of many thematic sinews lying beneath the story of Sybrant's initiation. Probably the novel's strongest theme concerns the struggle between two value systems once at war in the Hudson River Valley. The first, which Paulding calls "Doric," is associated with the rural Dutch and includes the values of simplicity, naturalness, and innocence; the second, called "Corinthian," is associated with the British, and includes those of ornamentation, artifice, and worldliness. For Paulding, everything from architecture to methods of warfare is related to these two congeries, with the first receiving his decided, but not exclusive, preference.

He first employs the term "Doric" in describing the homes of the colonial Dutchmen, which are characterized by clean lines and absence of embellishment; however, he soon extends the term to include a way of life, with an emphasis upon its wholesomeness. He writes of the Dutch settlers that "there was a certain doric simplicity in their mode of life, which has long since passed away, leaving behind what I sometimes feel inclined to doubt is but an inadequate compensation for its loss" (1:14). Referring to the changes wrought in American life over the course of time, he points out that "simplicity of manners is one of the great pillars of morality. It circumscribes our wants, and thus diminishes those besetting temptations to extravagance and dishonesty which originate in and receive their power from the love of dress, splendour, display, and luxury" (1:31). Becoming even more specific and perhaps self-revealing, he praises the rural pleasures of "those days of Doric innocence and simplicity" when picnicking and walking led only to "gentle and virtuous love," and he compares these to the urban decadence of "midnight revels, where dazzling lights, artificial splendours, seducing music, high-seasoned viands, and luxurious wines, pamper the senses into lascivious longings . . ." (1:46).

An entirely Doric approach to life, however, has its limitations, as Paulding uses Sybrant's boyhood teacher, Dominie Stettinius, to show. The Dominie is "a profound scholar, and a man of great piety as well as simplicity of character" (1:20); however, he is ignorant of "that knowledge of the world which, like small change, is essentia to the every day transactions of life" (1:21), particularly those between men and women. For this reason, he ill prepares Sybrant for his dealings with Catalina, with the Indians, and with the fashionable world of New York City. Nevertheless, to his credit, the Dominie perceives the bad influence exerted by the British upon the Dutch. We learn, for example, that Colonel Syndenham, after his arrival in the area, "was soon in special favour with high and low, rich and poor, young and old, with the single exception of the staid Dominie Stettinius, who penetrated his easiness of principles, and was not inclined to consider good manners an equivalent for good morals" (1:65).

Paulding presents the British soldiers, with their "fine Corinthian airs," as best suited to impress foolish women and naïve adolescents; his account of their actions and fate during the French and Indian War, though based in fact, serves well the purpose of indicting their values. Under Sir William's temporary command, they complain when he makes them doff their rich military dress, don Indian leggings, blacken their shiny gunbarrels, and crop their fine powdered hair. Later when General Abercrombie leads his men out of the fort to meet the Indians and the French, however, we learn that "the shores of Lake Champlain had never before witnessed so gallant an array of martial splendours" (2:108), and thus stupidly decked out in their "glittering finery," the British are no match for their stealthy enemies, who easily see them and kill over two thousand, with no losses of their own.

The hero and heroine of the novel are, of course, caught in the middle of the struggle between value systems. Catalina, though born a good Dutch girl and thus blessed with some Doric virtues, was bred at a boarding school in New York City, and as a consequence "she had lost much of the Doric, but had acquired a corresponding portion of the Corinthian" (1:29). This explains, of course, why she fails to appreciate Sybrant at first, and later forgets him when captivated by "the more piquant and gorgeous amusements of the capital" and "the society of the gay gallants in scarlet uniform" (1:29). Sybrant, on the other hand, was born the son of a British officer, and after being orphaned, was raised among his mother's Dutch relatives. When the novel begins he has the appearance and manners of "Doric roughness and simplicity" (1:27), but under the tutelage of a British baronet, Sir William Johnson, he gains sufficient knowledge of himself and the world to hone his character, earn the rank of major, and win Catalina's hand.

Throughout the novel, Paulding suggests, with his eighteenth-century voice, that the ideal society is one in which men live in harmony with their environment. Although a variety of experiences are necessary for the development of character, neither men nor women should stay long from their natural places. Hence, the British soldiers are an anomaly in the colonies, the Indians an anomaly out of the wilderness. Hans Pipe, Catalina's would-be assassin, provides support for this idea. He, it is suggested, has been corrupted by civilization. The satanic Indians in the novel are those who have adopted certain vices of white, civilized life, with intemperance, of course, the most outstanding example. Sir William tells Sybrant that an Indian woman is the ideal mate for a woodsman, because she is a natural part of the wilderness, an environment that would be alien to "a civilized European Lady" (1:110). His final advice to Sybrant: "If you ever come to live in the woods, marry a wood-nymph. You might as well bring a dancing-master here as a fine lady" (1:111).

In the event that one chooses to remain away from his native setting, however, as is the case with Sir William, the key to survival and to harmony, is to adapt oneself, rather than attempt to maintain an unnatural code of behavior. (The British are failures as fighting men because they attempt to fight an American war in an European manner.) Hence, Sir William learns the ways of the Indian and throws off many of the unnecessary trappings of civilized life. Similarly, Catalina can only achieve happiness, Paulding suggests, after she ceases her attempt to become a Great English Lady and learns to accept the provincialisms, and the young man, that are part of her natural environment.

Westward Ho!

The novel that appeared one year after *The Dutchman's Fireside* solidified Paulding's growing literary reputation (then at its height) and occasioned a number of laudatory summaries of his literary achievement. Brevoort wrote Irving that he had read *Westward Ho!* "with delight," adding, "It is the best of his works & not in my opinion surpassed by that of any other competitor of the day."[19] The reviewer for the *New-York Mirror* observed that Paulding "has increased in power as he has increased in years," and declared that he "may be now looked upon as a father in our letters." The *American Monthly Review*, after praising Paulding's contributions "to the establishment of a national literature," expressed admiration for "his genius, his vivid imagination, the classic elegance of his composition, and that rich and happy vein of humor, which runs through all his works." The highest tribute, however, came from the *New England Magazine*, whose reviewer wrote, "If we are to 'speak or die' which is the American novelist, we should name him in preference to Cooper. He has more wit, humor, and knowledge of character."[20]

Although *Westward Ho!* has not fared well at the hands of twentieth-century critics, there is much validity to the contemporary estimates of the novel. In only one respect is it decidedly weaker than *The Dutchman's Fireside*, and that is in its plot. Paulding, while writing the work, created the same problem for himself that he did with his other tale of the West, *The Backwoodsman*, for after telling the story of failure in the East and the journey to and successful settlement in the West, he found himself needing something more to write about to flesh out the story. In *The Backwoodsman*, he turned from Basil and his family to a gloomy deranged Indian prophet (the most fascinating character in the poem), and in *Westward Ho!* he turned from the Dangerfields, his pioneer family, to a gloomy, deranged young gentleman (who is, again, an interesting psychological study). As a result of this shift, the two parts of the narrative have different interests and different paces, which several critics have found unfortunate; nevertheless, Paulding skillfully uses a central theme concerning the psychological sources of happiness and misery to bind the two halves of the novel together.

The book begins with Colonel Cuthbert Dangerfield, a Virginia gentleman, struggling with indebtedness caused by his southern hospitality and his practice of raising only tobacco on his land, thus impoverishing it. When his primary creditor, a Scots merchant named Mactabb, starts dunning him, the Colonel seeks relief by gambling £40,000 on his famous, undefeated racehorse Barebones, who loses. Dangerfield must then visit Mactabb, who takes the deed to the Colonel's estate, pays his debts for him, gives him the balance of £5,000 to begin again, and commissions him to form a settlement on a large tract of land in Kentucky, "the dark and bloody ground" (1:95).

In the opening scenes, Paulding successfully conveys the manners, customs, and values of Virginian society, which he knew at first hand from his travels throughout the area in 1816. In addition, he creates a genial and high-spirited humor through his sketches of Mr. Ulysses Littlejohn, the Colonel's distant cousin, and Mrs. Dangerfield, a very wise, very supportive, very patient wife. The dialogues between her and her husband concerning their domestic and financial plight are both humorous and realistic, and they give the book a much faster early pace than that found in Paulding's other novels.

When the Dangerfields, with their young son and daughter, Littlejohn, and several devoted slaves who refuse their freedom, begin their westward journey, Paulding, who had not yet been west of the Alleghenies, draws much of his descriptive material from Reverend Timothy Flint's *Recollections of the Last Ten Years Passed in the Valley of the Mississippi* (1826). In his Preface, Paulding acknowledges "particular obligations" to Flint's book, and, as Arlin Turner has shown, Paulding's account of the land, the settlements, the rivers, the river boats, and the river people of the West are based on factual information found in Flint.[21]

Two of the characters who appear in the novel at this stage, however, Ambrose Bushfield and Samuel Hugg, are original frontier types of Paulding's own creation. Bushfield, whom the Dangerfields encounter in Pittsburgh as they begin their trek, resembles closely Paulding's lion of the West, Nimrod Wildfire, but he is more thoughtful and well developed. We are told that the independent, freedom-loving Bushfield left his native state of North Carolina because it got "so populous that he could hear his neighbor's dog bark" (1:68). He then joined Daniel Boone and was later captured and tortured by the Indians. Having visited North Carolina but finding it "so effeminate and corrupt that the men preferred featherbeds to dry leaves, and woolen coverlids to a sky blanket" (1:70), he has decided to return to "Old Kentuck." In appearance he is tall, muscular, graceful, and wears a buckskin shirt and raccoon-skin cap and leggins. In speech, moreover, he has the grandiloquence of the riproarer. "D'ye think," he asks, "I wouldn't have my way and my say, if an earthquake stood on one side and a flash of lightning on the other, and crossed their arms right before me, as much as to say, stand where you are?" (1:182–83).

Bushfield loves the "splendid independence of living in the woods, fifteen or twenty miles from any body" (1:84), where he can hear the bears and wolves "growling and howling round the house at night so beautifully" (1:184). He also enjoys hunting squirrels, and he explains, "When I want the skin of one of these fellers, I always shoot a *leetle* before his nose, and then the wind of the ball takes the varmint's breath clean away, and I don't hurt the fur" (1:172).

Paired with Bushfield as an engaging frontier creation is Hugg, captain and owner of the broadhorn that takes the Colonel and his family down the Ohio to their new home. Although Hugg, "a long-sided, weather-beaten oddity" (1:73), resembles Bushfield in his dialect, his rambling tall tale about a dandy he "smoked out" reveals him as a prototype of Mark Twain's garrulous old Simon Wheeler, whose rambling tale about Jim Smiley and his jumping frog initiated Twain's rise to fame thirty-three years later.

Once settled in the wilderness, with Bushfield as a neighbor, Colonel Dangerfield prospers, gaining in the course of ten years "the regard and respect of the settlers" in the region and becoming the wealthy "proprietor of half a dozen townships" (1:95). It is after this development then that a new protagonist, Dudley Rainsford, arrives in the town of Dangerfieldville astride a blooded horse and declares his intention of settling in the area. Like Koningsmarke, and even Sybrant at times, Rainsford resembles the typical Byronic hero. Though Paulding ridiculed "the club-footed lord,"[22] he was not disinclined to borrow from him. Rainsford is described as a dark, melancholy young man with a mysterious past who falls in love with the lovely, sensible Virginia Dangerfield, the Colonel's daughter. While taking a trip to New Orleans by himself, Rainsford encounters an earthquake which causes him to become abnormally superstitious; after his return he saves Virginia's life when her house burns down, and the two become engaged. He subsequently requests a one-year postponement of the wedding, however, for he fears he may soon go mad as his father and older brothers did at his same age.

After coming under the influence of a revival preacher, who insists that the sins of the father are visited upon the sons and that only by ridding oneself of all carnal lusts can one save his soul, Rainsford does go mad. Believing that his love for Virginia stands between him and salvation, he lures her to a secluded spot with the intention of sacrificing her, but although he raises his knife above her, he cannot bring himself to stab her and instead runs screaming into the forest. Some months later, he is discovered starved and raving by Bushfield and an Indian companion Black Warrior, who bring him back to Dangerfieldville, where he is confined and shows some signs of lucidity when Virginia visits him. He soon escapes, however, and disappears once more.

As a result of all this, Virginia becomes pale, thin, and sad. All of Paulding's heroines suffer because of the comings and goings of their true loves, and at times this seems to be their only function in life; however, Virginia, unlike Catalina Vancour in *The Dutchman's Fireside* and Jane Hammond in *The Old Continental*, receives Paulding's attention after the hero departs, and she does more than merely languish in the background. First, Virginia takes a trip on the Mississippi to regain her spirits. As she visits a village near St. Louis, her brother Leonard accidentally comes upon Rainsford, who is ragged, deranged, malnourished, and engaged in digging his own grave with the last of his strength, and after he is taken to an inn where a doctor declares he will soon die, Virginia insists upon trying to save his life. When her mother disapproves because Virginia herself is so weak, the daughter tells her that the weakest woman, animated by true affection, "can encounter fatigues, loss of rest, absence of food, yes, every privation of life, with a faith and perseverance to which men can never arrive" (2:164).

In her effort to save Rainsford, she succeeds, of course, with the help of Father Jacques, the local priest, who espouses a rational philosophy and rational religion that Rainsford responds to. "The difference between this rational old man," Paulding writes, "and the fiery-headed preacher of the terrors of the bottomless pit was, that the one goaded the apprehensive nervous being to madness, the other soothed him into a firm reliance on the mercies of the Supreme

Being" (2:172). After Rainsford's recovery, the novel then ends with a marriage and a description of the future prosperity of all.

As previously mentioned, twentieth-century critics have not thought highly of *Westward Ho!*, and the main criticism directed against it has been that it lacks unity. Alexander Cowie, for example, calls it a "none-too-happy blending of adventure and psychology." Similarly, Amos L. Herold declares that "though the novel begins as a story of adventure, it develops into an unpleasant psychological study, shifting its emphasis from the outer to the inner world." Offering praise he did not intend, Herold adds, ". . . it suffers from too much introspection and too little action, and reveals the author's literary kinship with Hawthorne."[23] Although the focus and pace of the novel indeed shift as it progresses, Paulding successfully links the story of Colonel Dangerfield and his losses with the story of Rainsford's psychological problems, by means of theme, rather than action or character.

In the opening scenes, Paulding has Mrs. Dangerfield introduce what will be the controlling idea of the book when she tells her husband not to despair about their financial plight. "My dear Cuthbert," she says, "this change of fortune will soon teach you how little, how very little, the blessings of life depend on mere situation. Guilt and remorse are the only lasting sources of misery" (1:37). The truth of this idea is developed and supported then not only through the positive example of the Colonel's financial recovery in the West, but also through the negative one of Rainsford's madness and misery caused by guilt about his grandfather's sin. (As a young loyalist in the Revolutionary War, his grandfather, in the heat of battle, gashed with his sword the head of an old gray-headed neighbor, a Whig, who cried out for quarter. For this act, he and his descendants were cursed with madness by the old man.) Rainsford's woe results from the words of the evangelical preacher who dwells with "savage exultation on the various dispensations of this world of guilt and misery" and convinces Rainsford he deserves to suffer "the wrath of the Almighty" (2:73).

Appropriately, Rainsford is cured by the ministrations of Virginia, for she, like her mother, perceives that outward circumstances are less important than one's state of mind and that the power of thought can often determine one's fate, can even save one's life when medical science insists there is no hope. "The true source of various maladies of mind and body," Virginia tells him, "is in the predisposition given by a presentiment that they will surely happen" (2:187).

Paulding uses not only his main characters but also some minor ones to develop this idea. For example, during a hunting expedition with Rainsford, Bushfield, and Littlejohn, the Indian Black Warrior (whose role, according to one critic, "is wholly external and has no bearing upon the structure of the novel")[24] explains that great medicine given by the Great Spirit causes him to shoot straight: "I go hunting, I shoot, shoot, shoot, no kill any thing, bad spirit won't let me, deer run away, birds fly away, no hit. Well, I go to conjurer, and he give me great medicine Great Spirit give him, and then when I fire, huh! down drop deer, bird, bear, every thing" (1:137). Littlejohn declares his disbelief in such unscientific medicine, but when a deer bounds past, "the charmed rifle of the Black Warrior," we are told, "arrested his course" (1:138).

The power of the human mind to alter one's physical condition for the better or worse is thus at the heart of the novel. The necessity of freeing oneself from guilt about the past is stressed both through the Colonel's need to pay his debts, so that he may prosper in the West, and through Rainsford's and Virginia's need to come to terms with the curse placed upon Rainsford's family, a curse that only gained efficacy through a belief in it. Although Hawthorne would treat such issues more skillfully and profoundly (particularly in *The House of the Seven Gables* [1851]), here Paulding succeeds in taking the historical romance beyond its conventional boundaries and revealing some significant truths about the human psyche. His own bout with madness induced by religious fanaticism gave him insights to draw upon, of course, and one only wishes he had used a less Byronic and more realistic protagonist to convey them.

All in all, *Westward Ho!* just misses being as fine a novel as *The Dutchman's Fireside.* If Paulding could have maintained the humor, suspense, and lively pace of the first half of the novel in the second half, it would have been. Nevertheless, even with its weaknesses, the book contains much of value, including realistic and original characters, much high-spirited good humor, and, most important, insightful psychological realism.

Chapter Nine

Conclusion

Examined in their totality, Paulding's life and works present much to admire; as Poe suggested, Paulding deserves praise "as a writer of pure and vigorous English, as a clear thinker, as a patriot, and as a man."[1] His character, though flawed by self-righteousness and prejudice, contained many sterling qualities: highmindedness, acuity, self-reliance, industry, a keen sense of humor, and, most important, courage in the face of formidable opposition. It is true, as has often been charged, that he wrote too hastily and he wrote for money; nevertheless, raised in bitter poverty, denied all but the most rudimentary formal education, he also, by means of his character and talent, educated himself, became a best-selling author admired by the finest writers in America, rose to one of the highest offices in the land, earned the friendship and respect of three presidents of the United States (Madison, Van Buren, and Jackson), and died a self-respecting and wealthy man.

As a patriot he displayed not a mindless, shallow chauvinism, but rather, a thoughtful, deep love of his country, acquired through witnessing the sufferings and hardships accompanying its birth. During a time when many accepted as deserved the disdain and contempt heaped upon America and Americans by influential British reviewers and travel-writers, his patriotism made him a leader in the use of humor and argumentation to defend his country and countrymen, at times, especially with his *John Bull in America*, even winning praise from the British for his efforts. In the process, however, he also became known, particularly among Federalists and anglophiles, as an ill-natured sneerer and was compared unfavorably with his fellow Salmagundian Irving, who was considered the epitome of genial sunniness.

Although such comparisons have depressed Paulding's literary reputation to this day, they have seldom been informed or fair, particularly when *Salmagundi* has served as the basis. As has been pointed out, it now seems certain that some of the weaker pieces in the series, containing vicious political satire which both authors later removed, were Irving's and that a number of the mellow, polished, personal essays which enhanced the series were Paulding's; however, for years just the opposite has been assumed. When Paulding published *Salmagundi* as part of his collected works, for example, he was called "a hack scribbler" by one reviewer, the venomous Park Benjamin, who declared, "As a whole, 'Salmagundi' is an admirable production; as a part of the writings of Paulding, it is a downright cheat." In what becomes a typical response to the collaboration, Benjamin urged, "Look into it, and if you find a good paper, be sure it is Washington Irving's; if you find a dull one, do not fail to ascribe it to Paulding."[2] Faced with such inequity, which even extended to his being called Irving's "jackal" by N. P. Willis, Paulding, though always quick to defend others, remained silent. For reasons known only to himself, Irving, the literary lion, also chose not to defend his friend publicly. He did, however, once observe in a letter to Brevoort, "There seems to be a pitiful and illiberal spirit indulged towards [Paulding] by the writers in our reviews and newspapers. What is the state of our literature that it can afford to treat with slight and contumely such a writer as Paulding—there is no one that has ever portrayed American scenery and characters with greater truth and beauty."[3]

As a writer, Paulding deserves credit, as Irving suggests, for his use of American materials and themes, which opened up valuable new literary territory for later writers. In *The Backwoodsman*, for example, his use of a lowly American character, the pioneer Basil, as his hero, though ridiculed at the time as unpoetic and vulgar, eventually led to many celebrations of the common man by others, most notably Whitman. His portrayal of the Indian in that poem was also one of the first in a long line of metrical treatments that detailed the bitterness and nobility of that vanishing American as he confronted the forces of white agrarian civilization. Similarly, his descriptions of Hudson River Valley scenery in this poem and in his other works contributed to the emergence of the Hudson River School of painters, a number of whom, including Asher Durand, John G. Chapman, and Robert W. Weir, drew inspiration from him.

Paulding's literary criticism, his most important work, though based upon eighteenth-century standards, was years ahead of its time and anticipated the literary nationalism of Emerson, Melville, and Whitman and the defense of literary realism by Twain, Howells, and James. His critical insistence that American drama and fiction be original and national, that it deal with the essence of life, with a firm sense of place, of time, of human speech and human behavior, plus his idea that this fidelity to observed reality could clarify one's moral vision, marked the beginning of a new, serious attitude toward the creation of American literature. Not Irving, not Cooper, and perhaps not even Poe, as gifted a critic as he was, saw so clearly, cared so deeply about, and articulated so well the ways in which American writers could and would establish a national literature of uniqueness and value.

Much of Paulding's own poetry, drama, and fiction, with its signs of hasty composition and inadequate revision, fails to meet his critical standards; his best writings, however, by which he deserves to be judged, do meet them and constitute valuable contributions to the American literary development he called for. His famous play *The Lion of the West*, for example, not only achieved immense popularity, thanks in part to the acting skills of James H. Hackett, but it also, through the featuring of the tall-talking frontiersman and the believable rendering of his humorous idiom, helped form a taproot of American folklore and native American humor.

Similarly, his best short stories and novels, with their portrayals of the New York Dutch, the Indian, and frontier types, with their treatment of fresh American themes, compose a small body of writings enriched with innovative humor, local color, realism, and, at times, psychological depth. As such they gained him the respect of his most talented literary peers. In 1836, for example, Poe publicly cited Paulding as a stylist excelled by "certainly no American, and possible no living writer of England"[4] and sought his help in placing a volume of his short stories. Although unable to help, Paulding advised the younger writer to follow his satiric bent and to try writing a long work. The apparent result, published one year later, was *The Narrative of Arthur Gordon Pym.*[5] In 1839, Simms addressed Paulding "as one among the most successful of our native authors,—as indeed, one of the fathers of our forest literature,—a leading Pioneer"[6] and proceeded to dedicate his novel *The Damsel of Darien* to him. In 1840, Hawthorne wrote in a letter to Paulding, "I cannot but feel it one of my birthrights to address Mr. Paulding; who has made himself the admired and familiar friend of every reader in the land."[7]

Some ten years later, when Hawthorne wrote *The Scarlet Letter*, he evidently used Paulding's "The Dumb Girl" as a source. Finally, in January 1850, one month before Hawthorne's novel appeared, Cooper, Paulding's friend, kindred spirit, and probable debtor, ranked him third, behind Bryant and Irving, on his list of living American writers who had created a literature that "cannot be put down." "We have got a foothold," Cooper declared, "and by God's blessing we will maintain it."[8]

In contrast to such important contemporary respect, in 1867 a reviewer for the *Nation*, in response to William I. Paulding's apologetic memoir of his father, declared, "[Paulding] does not deserve a long biography, nor elaborate criticism, nor, briefly, remembrance. And in fact he has been very well forgotten."[9] As a growing number of modern critics have realized, such is not the case. Although many, too many, of his writings are mere journalistic fare, although weaknesses in conception or execution mar his efforts in a multitude of genres, Paulding nevertheless wrote a body of literary criticism and at least six works (*Salmagundi, John Bull in America, The Backwoodsman, The Lion of the West*, "Cobus Yerks," and *The Dutchman's Fireside*) that deserve to be read by anyone interested in the origins of American critical thought or the mainstream of American literary history.

Notes and References

Chapter One

1. Amos L. Herold, *James Kirke Paulding: Versatile American* (New York, 1926), pp. 1–2; Floyd C. Watkins, "James Kirke Paulding: Humorist and Critic of American Life" (Ph.D. diss, Vanderbilt, 1952), p. 137; and Kendall B. Taft, *Minor Knickerbockers* (New York, 1947), pp. xcv–xcvi, have pointed this out.

2. Unless otherwise noted, the biographical details in this chapter are drawn from *The Letters of James Kirke Paulding*, ed. Ralph M. Aderman (Madison, 1962); Herold, *Paulding*; William I. Paulding's *Literary Life of James K. Paulding* (New York, 1867), and Paulding's autobiographical sketch on file in the Duyckinck Papers in the New York Public Library and also appended, in typescript, to Watkins's dissertation, pp. 320–41.

3. *Souvenir of the Revolutionary Soldiers' Monument Dedication at Tarrytown, N.Y., October 19th, 1894*, comp. Marcius D. Raymond (Tarrytown, 1894), p. 159.

4. William I. Paulding, *Literary Life*, p. 24.

5. See Egbert Benson, *Vindication of the Captors of Major Andre* (New York: Kirk and Mercein, 1817), pp. 9–13.

6. William I. Paulding, *Literary Life*, p. 19.

7. See Ralph M. Aderman, "James Kirke Paulding's Literary Income," *Bulletin of the New York Public Library* 64 (March 1960):117–129, and Herold, *Paulding*, p. 140.

8. William I. Paulding, *Literary Life*, pp. 26, 20.

9. Ibid., p. 26.

10. *Tales of the Good Woman, by A Doubtful Gentleman*, 2 vols. (New York, 1836), 1:185.

11. William I. Paulding, *Literary Life*, p. 26.

12. See Eleanor Bryce Scott, "Early Literary Clubs in New York City," *American Literature* 5 (March 1933):3–16.

13. William I. Paulding, *Literary Life*, p. 30.

14. For the fullest account of the activities of the "Lads," see Pierre M. Irving, *The Life and Letters of Washington Irving*, 4 vols. (New York: Putnam, 1864), 1:164–72.

15. Quoted by Aderman in *Letters*, p. 27.

16. *The New Mirror for Travellers, and Guide to the Springs, by an Amateur* (New York, 1828), p. 109.

17. See Stanley T. Williams, *The Life of Washington Irving*, 2 vols.

(New York: Oxford University Press, 1935), 2:264.

18. *Letters of Washington Irving to Henry Brevoort,* ed. George S. Hellman, 2 vols. (New York: G. P. Putnam's Sons, 1918), 2:99.

19. Ibid., 2:123.

20. Aderman, Introduction to *Letters*, p. xvii.

21. Washington Irving, *The Sketch Book*, ed. Haskell Springer (Boston: Twayne Publishers, 1977), p. 49.

22. *Salmagundi, Second Series, by Launcelot Langstaff, Esq.*, 2 vols. (New York, 1835), 2:270.

23. See Harold E. Hall, "James Kirke Paulding: A Pioneer in American Fiction" (Ph.D. diss., University of Pennsylvania, 1953), pp. 27–28.

24. Herold, *Paulding*, p. 66.

25. Edgar Allan Poe, "Paulding's Washington," *Southern Literary Messenger* 2 (May 1836):396–99.

26. See William I. Paulding, *Literary Life*, p. 263, on doubt as to year of publication.

27. N. P. Willis, "Paulding the Author Disinterred," *Southern Literary Messenger* 5 (June 1839):415–17.

28. Quoted in Williams, *Irving*, 2:68.

29. William I. Paulding, *Literary Life*, pp. 287–88.

30. William Dean Howells, "The Literary Life of James K. Paulding," *Atlantic Monthly* 20 (July 1867):124.

31. William I. Paulding, *Literary Life*, pp. iii–iv.

Chapter Two

1. See *Washington Irving's Contributions to "The Corrector,"* Minnesota Monographs in the Humanities, no. 3, ed. Martin Roth (Minneapolis: University of Minnesota Press, 1968).

2. E. A. Duyckinck's Editor's Preface to *Salmagundi, Irving's Works* (New York, 1860), pp. 12–13, and Herold, *Paulding*, p. 35, provide accounts of Longworth's activities.

3. *Oldstyle; Salmagundi*, by Washington Irving, ed. Bruce I. Granger and Martha Hartzog (Boston: Twayne Publishers, 1977), p. 68.

4. Pierre M. Irving, *Life and Letters*, 1:177.

5. Quoted in Duyckinck's note to 1860 *Salmagundi*, pp. 92–93.

6. Ibid., pp. 93–94.

7. Williams, *Irving*, 2:265.

8. Duyckinck note, p. 94.

9. Williams, *Irving*, 1:79.

10. Ibid., 2:263.

11. Historical Note to 1977 *Salmagundi*, p. 321.

12. Williams, *Irving*, 2:268.

13. Ibid., 1:83.

14. William I. Paulding, *Literary Life*, pp. 38–39.
15. Pierre M. Irving, *Life and Letters*, 1:179.
16. Richard H. Dana, a review in *North American Review* 9 (September 1819):334.
17. John Lambert, *Travels Through Lower Canada, and the United States of North America, in the Years 1806, 1807, & 1808*, 3 vols. (London: R. Phillips, 1810), 2:98.
18. See Herold, *Paulding*, p. 32.
19. Quoted in Pierre M. Irving, *Life and Letters*, 1:212–13.
20. *Letters of Irving to Brevoort*, 2:99.
21. William I. Paulding, *Literary Life*, p. 39.
22. See *North American Review* 28 (January 1829):116; *Quarterly Review* 31 (March 1825):475; and *New England Magazine* 9 (July 1835):130.
23. See Textual Commentary in 1977 *Salmagundi*, p. 405.
24. See List of Rejected Substantives in 1977 *Salmagundi*, pp. 479–80.
25. Textual Commentary, p. 403.
26. Ibid., p. 408.
27. John Neal, two articles in *Blackwood's Magazine*: "American Writers IV," 17 (January 1825):61; "American Writers V," 17 (February 1825):199.
28. Bruce I. Granger, Historical Note, 1977 *Salmagundi*, p. 324.
29. 1860 *Salmagundi*, pp. 9–10.
30. For an analysis of Willis's motives, see "Letters from New York," *Southern Literary Messenger* 5 (September 1839):630.
31. Willis, "Paulding . . . Disinterred," p. 416.
32. Fred Lewis Pattee, *The First Century of American Literature 1770–1870* (New York: D. Appleton-Century, 1935), pp. 292–93; Van Wyck Brooks, *The World of Washington Irving* (New York: E. P. Dutton, 1944), pp. 255, 179.
33. *Letters of Irving to Brevoort*, 2:123.
34. See Perry Miller, *The Raven and the Whale: The War of Words and Wits in the Era of Poe and Melville* (1955; reprint ed., Westport, Conn.: Greenwood Press, 1976), pp. 67–68.
35. The 1835 Harpers edition of the series contains only thirteen numbers because Paulding removed No. 12 for July 22, 1820, keeping only one essay from it, and he condensed No. 15 for September 2, 1820, and combined it with the preceding number. Thus the 1835 edition (which appears to be a direct reprint because the original dates of publication are retained) is actually a revised edition that is six essays and some 120 pages shorter than the rare 1819–20 edition. I am indebted to my colleague Norman Grabo for bringing this previously unnoticed bibliographic fact to my attention.

36. *Letters of Henry Brevoort to Washington Irving*, ed. George S. Hellman (New York: G. P. Putnam's Sons, 1918), pp. 111–12.
37. Ibid., p. 124.
38. Amos L. Herold, "Paulding's Literary Theories," *Bulletin of the New York Public Library* 66 (April 1962):236.

Chapter Three

1. Evert A. and George L. Duyckinck, *The Cyclopaedia of American Literature* (Philadelphia: William Rutter & Co., 1877), p. 5.
2. See Floyd C. Watkins, "The Political Career of James Kirke Paulding," *Emory University Quarterly* 6 (December 1950):225–35.
3. *Letters of Irving to Brevoort*, 1:111.
4. *Letters of Brevoort to Irving*, p. 237.
5. Informative accounts of the Paper War will be found in Jane Louise Mesick, *The English Traveller in America, 1785–1835* (1922; reprint ed., Westport, Conn.: Greenwood Press, 1970), pp. 270–98; Allan Nevins, *American Social History as Recorded by British Travellers* (New York: Henry Holt & Co., 1923), pp. 3–26 and 111–38; and Dennis Duane Gartner, Historical Introduction to "A Critical Edition and Study of James Kirke Paulding's 'The Diverting History of John Bull and Brother Jonathan' " (Ph.D. diss., University of Wisconsin, 1972), pp. 162–82.
6. Nevins, *American Social History*, p. 10.
7. *Quarterly Review* 2 (November 1809):311.
8. "The Bucktails" in *American Comedies*, by J. K. Paulding and William Irving Paulding (Philadelphia, 1847), p. 25.
9. *Quarterly Review* 10 (January 1814):501, 502, 516, 519, 521, 522.
10. *Letters from the South, Written during an Excursion in the Summer of 1816*, 2 vols. (New York, 1817), 2:134–35, 135–36, 138.
11. See Williams, *Irving*, 1:192.
12. Irving, *The Sketch Book*, pp. 48–49.
13. Sydney Smith, "America," *Edinburgh Review* 32 (January 1820): 79–80.
14. *Westward Ho!*, 2 vols. (New York, 1832), 2:119.
15. See Joyce Henry, "Five More Essays by James Kirke Paulding?" *Papers of the Bibliographical Society of America* 66 (Third Quarter 1972):310–21.
16. Gartner Critical Edition, p. 1.
17. See ibid., p. 185.
18. See George E. Hastings, "John Bull and His American Descendants," *American Literature* 1 (March 1929):40–68; Gartner Critical Edition, pp. 194–200.
19. Herold, *Paulding*, p. 40.
20. Luther S. Mansfield, "Diversity and Innovation in the Middle States,"

Literary History of the United States: History, ed. Robert E. Spiller et al., 3d ed., rev. (New York: Macmillan, 1963), p. 271.

21. See Watkins, "James Kirke Paulding," pp. 89–94.

22. Ibid., p. 216.

23. *John Bull in America; or, The New Munchausen* (New York, 1825), p. 28.

24. Charles William Janson, *The Stranger in America, 1793–1806*, introduction by Carl S. Driver (1807; reprint ed., New York: The Press of the Pioneers, 1935), pp. xi–xix.

25. Quoted in William B. Cairns, *British Criticism of American Writings, 1815–1833*, University of Wisconsin Studies in Language and Literature, no. 14 (Madison, 1922), p. 205.

26. Quoted in ibid., p. 205.

27. John Neal, "Late American Books," *Blackwood's Magazine* 18 (September 1825):328.

28. Herold, *Paulding*, p. 63; Watkins, "James Kirke Paulding," p. 89.

Chapter Four

1. J. Albert Robbins describes this book in "Some Unrecorded Poems of James Kirke Paulding: An Annotated Check-List," *Studies in Bibliography* 3 (1950):229–40.

2. James D. Hart, *The Popular Book: A History of America's Literary Taste* (Berkeley and Los Angeles: University of California Press, 1963), p. 69.

3. Samuel Goodrich, *Recollections of a Lifetime, or Men and Things I Have Seen*, 2 vols. (1856; reprint ed., Detroit: Gale Research, 1967), 2:100–101.

4. Mark Twain, *Life on the Mississippi*, ed. Albert Bigelow Paine (1883; reprint ed., New York: Gabriel Wells, 1923), p. 375.

5. Thomas O'Donnell points this out in "*Koningsmarke*: Paulding vs. Scott in 1823," *American Transcendental Quarterly*, no. 24 (Fall 1974), p. 16, n. 14.

6. *The Lay of the Scottish Fiddle: A Poem in Five Cantos, Supposed to be written by W—— S——, Esq.*, First American, from the Fourth Edinburgh Edition (London, 1814), p. 220.

7. See Ralph M. Aderman, "Publication Dates of Three Early Works by James Kirke Paulding," *Papers of the Bibliographical Society of America* 59 (First Quarter 1965):49.

8. This account of British activities on the Chesapeake is drawn from Benson J. Lossing, *The Pictorial Field-Book of the War of 1812* (New York: Harper & Brothers, 1869), pp. 667–97, 916–77; Gilbert Byron, *The War of 1812 on the Chesapeake Bay* (Baltimore: Maryland Historical

Society, 1964); and John K. Mahon, *The War of 1812* (Gainesville: University of Florida Press, 1972), pp. 109–22.

9. Quoted in Lossing, *Pictorial*, p. 684.

10. See Mahon, *War of 1812*, p. 115.

11. See, for example, the account of the defense of Washington in ibid., pp. 297–301.

12. Washington Irving, a review in *Analectic Magazine* 2 (September 1813):223–24.

13. See Pierre M. Irving, *Life and Letters*, 1:310–12.

14. Introduction to *Lay of the Scottish Fiddle*, pp. iv–v.

15. Review in *Quarterly Review* 10 (January 1814):464–67.

16. Quoted in Cairns, *British Criticism*, p. 173.

17. *The Backwoodsman* (Philadelphia, 1818), p. 19.

18. See James T. Callow, *Kindred Spirits: Knickerbocker Writers and American Artists, 1807–1855* (Chapel Hill: University of North Carolina Press, 1967), pp. 87–88, 117–118, 190.

19. The two are reproduced in John K. Howat's *The Hudson River and Its Painters* (New York: Viking, 1972), plates 49 and 40.

20. "G.," review in *American Monthly Magazine and Critical Review* 4 (January 1819):165.

21. Quoted in William I. Paulding, *Literary Life,* p. 96.

22. Quoted in ibid., pp. 96–97.

23. Quoted in Herold, *Paulding*, p. 141.

24. Quoted in Cairns, *British Criticism*, pp. 164, 164, 165.

25. Spiller, *Literary History of the United States*, pp. 272–73.

26. Roy Harvey Pearce, *The Savages of America: A Study of the Indian and the Idea of Civilization* (1953; rev. ed. Baltimore: Johns Hopkins University Press, 1965), pp. 188, 188–89.

27. G. Harrison Orians, "The Rise of Romanticism, 1805–1855," in *Transitions in American Literary History*, ed. Harry Hayden Clark (Durham, N.C.: Duke University Press, 1953), p. 214. See also Orians's *The Cult of the Vanishing American: A Century View: 1834–1934* (Toledo, Ohio: H. J. Chittenden Company, 1934), pp. 3–10.

28. Melvin Rosser Mason, "The Uncollected Stories of James Kirke Paulding: An Annotated Edition," (Ph.D. diss., University of Texas, 1958), p. 36.

29. *Letters of Brevoort to Irving*, pp. 26, 31.

30. Irving, *The Sketch Book*, p. 225.

31. Ibid., p. 235.

32. "The Eve of Saint Andrew" (1830) in Mason, "The Uncollected Stories," p. 283.

33. James Grant Wilson, *Bryant and His Friends: Some Reminiscences of the Knickerbocker Writers* (New York: Fords, Howard, and Hulbert, 1886), pp. 150–51.

Chapter Five

1. See John J. McCloskey, "The Campaign of Periodicals after the War of 1812 for National American Literature," *PMLA* 50 (March 1935): 262–73.
2. See Aderman, "Publication Dates of Three Early Works," p. 50.
3. *The United States and England* (New York, 1815), p. 95.
4. Walter Channing, two articles: "Essay on American Language and Literature," *North American Review* 1 (September 1815):312–13; "Reflections on the Literary Delinquency of America," *North American Review* 2 (November 1815):39.
5. See Robert E. Streeter, "Association Psychology and Literary Nationalism in the *North American Review*, 1815–1825," *American Literature* 17 (November 1945):243–54; and Robert E. Spiller, Explanatory Notes in *The American Literary Revolution, 1783–1837*, ed. Robert E. Spiller (Garden City, N.Y.: Doubleday, 1967), pp. 109–11.
6. Irving, *The Sketch Book*, p. 49.
7. "York Town: An Historical Romance," *American Quarterly Review* 2 (September 1827):32.
8. *A Sketch of Old England*, 2 vols. (New York, 1822), 2:148, 129, 125.
9. Herold, "Paulding's Literary Theories," p. 239.
10. Louis D. Owens points this out in "James K. Paulding and the Foundations of American Realism," *Bulletin of the New York Public Library* 79 (Autumn 1975):40–50.
11. Eugene Current-Garcia and Walton R. Patrick, *Realism and Romanticism in Fiction: An Approach to the Novel* (Chicago: Scott, Foresman, 1962), p. 14.
12. *Criticism and Fiction and Other Essays by W. D. Howells*, ed. Clara Marburg Kirk and Rudolf Kirk (New York: New York University Press, 1959), p. 20; "Fenimore Cooper's Literary Offenses" in *The Portable Mark Twain*, ed. Bernard DeVoto (New York: Viking, 1946), pp. 542–43; "The Art of Fiction" in *Henry James: Selected Fiction*, ed. Leon Edel (New York: Dutton, 1964), p. 587.
13. Alexander Cowie, *The Rise of the American Novel* (New York, 1948), p. 197.
14. G. Harrison Orians, "The Romance Ferment after *Waverley*," *American Literature* 3 (January 1932):413.
15. See Hart, *The Popular Book*, pp. 304–5.
16. Introduction to *The Dutchman's Fireside*, ed. Thomas F. O'Donnell (New Haven, Conn.: College and University Press, 1966), p. 11; Spiller, *Literary History of the United States*, p. 272.
17. Ralph M. Aderman first identified these reviews as Paulding's in "James Kirke Paulding's Literary Income." See also Aderman's "Contribu-

tors to the *American Quarterly Review*, 1827–1833," *Studies in Bibliography* 14 (1961):163–76, and "Paulding's Contributions to American Magazines," *Studies in Bibliography* 17 (1964):141–51.

18. "American Drama," *American Quarterly Review* 1 (June 1827): 333–34.

19. Arthur Hobson Quinn, *A History of the American Drama: From the Beginning to the Civil War*, 2d. ed. (New York: F. S. Crofts, 1944), p. 202.

20. Ibid., p. 391.

21. "Dramatic Literature," *American Quarterly Review* 8 (September 1830):152.

22. Nelson F. Adkins, "James K. Paulding's *Lion of the West*," *American Literature* 3 (November 1931):249.

23. See Floyd C. Watkins, "James K. Paulding's Early Ring-Tailed Roarer," *Southern Folklore Quarterly* 15 (September 1951):183–87, and *Letters*, p. 34. Joseph J. Arpad, "The Fight Story: Quotation and Originality in Native American Humor," *Journal of the Folklore Institute* 10 (1973):141–72, speculates on other possible sources of one of the tales Paulding recorded.

24. Owens, "James K. Paulding and the Foundations of American Realism," pp. 48–49.

25. F. O. Matthiessen, *American Renaissance: Art and Expression in the Age of Emerson and Whitman* (New York: Oxford University Press, 1941), p. ix.

26. *The Puritan and His Daughter*, 2 vols. (New York, 1849), 1:5.

27. Herold, "Paulding's Literary Theories," p. 243.

28. William Charvat, *The Origins of American Critical Thought, 1810–1835* (Philadelphia: University of Pennsylvania Press, 1936), pp. 201–2.

29. Ibid., p. 92.

30. Ibid., pp. 122–23; see also the discussion of diction, pp. 132–33.

31. Ibid., pp. 143, 149.

32. Although Aderman published his list of Paulding's anonymous contributions in 1964, subsequent studies of American criticism have overlooked it. In his excellent collection of primary materials, *The American Literary Revolution, 1783–1837*, Robert E. Spiller includes Paulding's essay "American Drama" but tentatively and erroneously credits Robert Walsh with its authorship. More recently, Michael Davitt Bell, in *The Development of American Romance: The Sacrifice of Relation* (Chicago: University of Chicago Press, 1980), not only attributes the "York Town" article to an anonymous critic, but uses it to show that "many commentators agreed with Paulding about the necessity of realism in American romance, but they were far less happy about it than he was" (p. 19).

Chapter Six

1. See Pierre M. Irving, *Life and Letters*, 1:35–36.
2. See *Letters*, p. 171.
3. Herold, *Paulding*, p. 99; *Cyclopaedia of American Literature*, p. 4.
4. Watkins, "James Kirke Paulding," p. 80.
5. Quoted in William I. Paulding, *Literary Life*, p. 218.
6. Quoted in Adkins, "Paulding's *Lion of the West*," pp. 249–50.
7. *The Lion of the West*, ed. James N. Tidwell (Stanford, Calif., 1954), p. 27.
8. See Joseph J. Arpad, "John Wesley Jarvis, James Kirk [*sic*] Paulding, and Colonel Nimrod Wildfire," *New York Folklore Quarterly* 21 (June 1965):92–106.
9. Quoted in William I. Paulding, *Literary Life*, pp. 218–19.
10. See Tidwell's Introduction to *Lion of the West*, pp. 7–8.
11. An outline of the original version that appeared in *The Morning Courier and New York Enquirer*, April 27, 1831, is reprinted in Adkins, "Paulding's *Lion of the West*," pp. 257–58.
12. Quoted in ibid., p. 252.
13. See Henry, "Five More Essays," pp. 310–21.
14. See Tidwell, Introduction, p. 11.
15. Quoted in William I. Paulding, *Literary Life*, p. 219.
16. A portrait of Hackett as Wildfire is reproduced on the first page of Tidwell's edition of the play.
17. Melvin R. Mason, "*The Lion of the West*: Satire on Davy Crockett and Frances Trollope," *SCMLA Studies* 29 (Winter 1969):143–45.
18. See Watkins, "James Kirke Paulding's Early Ring-Tailed Roarer," p. 185.
19. Walter Blair and Hamlin Hill discuss the "reputable" and "subversive" traditions in *America's Humor: From Poor Richard to Doonesbury* (New York: Oxford University Press, 1978), pp. 155–221.
20. In his influential study, *Form and Fable in American Fiction* (1961; reprint ed., New York: Oxford University Press, 1965), Daniel C. Hoffman disparages the play and its humor; he attributes a subversive anti-intellectualism to Wildfire, whom he sees not as a caricature, but as an accurate portrayal of David Crockett, whose appeal "as politician," Hoffman declares, "is dangerous and demagogic" (p. 71).

Chapter Seven

1. Watkins, "James Kirke Paulding," p. 319.
2. *The First Century of American Literature, 1770–1870*, p. 400.
3. Herold, *Paulding*, p. 72.

4. "Cobus Yerks," *The Book of Saint Nicholas: Translated from the Original Dutch of Dominie Nicholas Aegidius Oudenarde* (New York, 1836 or 1837), p. 79.

5. See Herold, *Paulding*, pp. 82–84, and Louis Owens, "Paulding's 'The Dumb Girl,' A Source of *The Scarlet Letter*," *Nathaniel Hawthorne Journal*, 1974, pp. 240–49.

6. "The Dumb Girl," *Tales of the Good Woman*, p. 211.

7. *Passages from the American Notebooks of Nathaniel Hawthorne* (Boston and New York: Houghton Mifflin, 1868), p. 25.

8. See W. T. Conklin, "Paulding's Prose Treatment of Types and Frontier Lore Before Cooper," *University of Texas Studies in English*, no. 19 (July 8, 1939), pp. 163–71.

9. "The Adventures of Henry Bird," in Mason, "The Uncollected Short Stories," p. 33.

10. Conklin, "Paulding's Prose Treatment," p. 167.

11. Herold, *Paulding*, p. 66.

Chapter Eight

1. *Koningsmarke: or, Old Times in the New World*, 2 vols. (New York, 1836), 2:63–64.

2. Review in *Minerva* 2 (November 1, 1823):238–39.

3. Review in *New-York Mirror* 1 (November 1, 1823):108.

4. These three British reviews, along with six others of like nature, are quoted in Cairns, *British Criticism*, pp. 201–4.

5. Vernon L. Parrington, *Main Currents in American Thought: Volume Two, 1800–1860, The Romantic Revolution in America* (New York, 1927), p. 212; Albert Keiser, *The Indian in American Literature* (New York: Oxford University Press, 1933), pp. 46, 48–49; Cowie, *The Rise of the American Novel*, p. 187; Hall, "James Kirke Paulding," p. 42.

6. Herold, *Paulding*, pp. 96–97; James Holman Robertson, "James Kirke Paulding: A Study in Literary Nationalism" (Ph.D. diss, Michigan, 1950), p. 342; O'Donnell, "*Koningsmarke*: Paulding vs. Scott in 1823," p. 14.

7. *The Dutchman's Fireside, A Tale*, 2 vols. (New York, 1837), 1:5.

8. Dorothy Dondore points out some of these borrowings in "The Debt of Two Dyed-in-the-Wool Americans to Mrs. Grant's Memoirs: Cooper's *Satanstoe* and Paulding's *The Dutchman's Fireside*," *American Literature* 12 (March 1940):52–58.

9. *The Letters and Journals of James Fenimore Cooper,* ed. James Franklin Beard, 6 vols. (Cambridge, Mass.: Belknap Press of Harvard University Press, 1960), 2:151–52.

10. Hart, *The Popular Book*, p. 305; Herold, *Paulding*, p. 151.

11. Quoted in Robertson, "James Kirke Paulding," p. 16.

12. *The Letters of Cooper*, 2:150.
13. Quoted in Cairns, *British Criticism*, p. 206.
14. Ibid., p. 207.
15. Herold, *Paulding*, p. 100; Parrington, *Main Currents*, p. 213; "Introduction," *The Dutchman's Fireside*, 1966, p. 18.
16. Arthur Hobson Quinn, *American Fiction: An Historical and Critical Survey* (New York: Appleton-Century-Crofts, 1936), p. 47; Robertson, "James Kirke Paulding," pp. 285–86, 324; Watkins, "James Kirke Paulding," p. 24.
17. Leland S. Person, Jr., "James Kirke Paulding: Myth and the Middle Ground," *Western American Literature* 16 (Spring 1981): 54, 39.
18. Cowie, *Rise*, p. 191.
19. *Letters of Brevoort to Irving*, p. 262.
20. Reviews in *New-York Mirror* 10 (October 20, 1832):122; *American Monthly Review* 3 (January 1833):55–56; *New England Magazine* 3 (November 1832):424.
21. Arlin Turner, "James Kirke Paulding and Timothy Flint," *Mississippi Valley Historical Review* 34 (June 1947):105–11.
22. *The Dutchman's Fireside*, 2:56.
23. Cowie, *Rise*, p. 193; Herold, *Paulding*, p. 104.
24. Nelson F. Adkins, "A Study of James K. Paulding's *Westward Ho!*" *American Collector* 3 (March 1927):227.

Chapter Nine

1. Edgar Allan Poe, review in *Southern Literary Messenger* 2 (April 1836):338.
2. Park Benjamin, "Literary Humbug," *New England Magazine* 9 (July 1835):130.
3. *Letters of Irving to Brevoort*, 2:122–23.
4. Edgar Allan Poe, "Paulding's Washington," *Southern Literary Messenger* 2 (May 1836):399.
5. See Herold, *Paulding*, pp. 74–77.
6. *The Letters of William Gilmore Simms*, ed. Mary C. Simms Oliphant et al., 5 vols. (Columbia: University of South Carolina Press, 1953), 2:144.
7. Quoted in Ralph M. Aderman, "The Case of James Cook: A Study of Political Influence in 1840," *Essex Institute Historical Collection* 92 (1956):63.
8. *Cooper's Letters*, 6:108.
9. Review in the *Nation* 4 (May 30, 1867):431.

Selected Bibliography

PRIMARY SOURCES

1. Selected Literary Criticism (in chronological order)

"American Drama." *American Quarterly Review* 1 (June 1827):331–57.

"York Town: An Historical Romance." *American Quarterly Review* 2 September 1827):19–46.

"Dramatic Literature." *American Quarterly Review* 8 (September 1830): 134–61.

"National Literature." Revised in *Salmagundi, Second Series* (1835), 2:265–72. Entitled "The Wreck of Genius" in *Salmagundi, Second Series* (1819–20), 3:264–88.

2. Novels (in chronological order)

Koningsmarke, The Long Finne, A Story of the New World. 2 vols. New York: Charles Wiley, 1823. *Koningsmarke: or, Old Times in the New World.* Revised ed. 2 vols. New York: Harper & Brothers, 1836.

The Dutchman's Fireside, A Tale. 2 vols. New York: Harper & Brothers, 1831. 5th ed. 2 vols. New York: Harper & Brothers, 1837. Edited by Thomas H. O'Donnell. Reprint ed. New Haven, Conn.: College and University Press, 1966.

Westward Ho! 2 vols. New York: J. and J. Harper, 1832. Reprint ed. Grosse Pointe, Mich.: Scholarly Press, 1968.

The Old Continental; or, The Price of Liberty. 2 vols. New York: Paine and Burgess, 1846.

The Puritan and His Daughter. 2 vols. New York: Baker & Scribner, 1849.

3. Plays (in chronological order)

The Bucktails, or Americans in England. Written circa 1813. Not produced. Published in *American Comedies.* Philadelphia: Carey & Hart, 1847.

The Lion of the West; or a Trip to Washington. Written 1830. Produced 1831. Edited by James N. Tidwell. Stanford, Calif.: Stanford University Press, 1954.

4. Selected Short Stories (in chronological order)

"The Adventures of Henry Bird." *Analectic Magazine* 6 (October 1815): 295–301.

"The Little Dutch Sentinel of the Manhadoes." *Atlantic Souvenir*, Philadelphia, 1827, pp. 154–93.
"Cobus Yerks." *Atlantic Souvenir*, Philadelphia, 1828, pp. 192–206.
"The Dumb Girl." In: *Chronicles of the City of Gotham* (New York: G. and C. and H. Carvill, 1830), pp. 231–70.
"Childe Roeliff's Pilgrimage." In: *Tales of Glauber-Spa.* 2 vols. (New York: J. and J. Harper, 1832), 1:109–89.

5. Essay Collections (in chronological order)

Salmagundi; or, the Whim-Whams and Opinions of Launcelot Langstaff, Esq. and Others. 2 vols. New York: D. Longworth. 1807–1808. Edited by Bruce I. Granger and Martha Hartzog. Boston: Twayne Publishers, 1977.
Letters from the South, Written during an Excursion in the Summer of 1816. 2 vols. New York: James Eastburn & Company, 1817. Reprint ed. New York: AMS Press, 1973.
Salmagundi, Second Series, by Launcelot Langstaff, Esq. 3 vols. Philadelphia and New York: M. Thomas; J. Haly & C. Thomas, 1819–1820. Revised ed. 2 vols. New York: Harper & Brothers, 1835. Reprinted from the 1835 ed. New York: AMS Press, 1974.

6. Book-Length Poems (in chronological order)

The Lay of the Scottish Fiddle: A Tale of Havre de Grace, supposed to be written by Walter Scott, Esq. New York and Philadelphia: Inskeep & Bradford; Bradford & Inskeep, 1813. *The Lay of the Scottish Fiddle: A Poem in Five Cantos, Supposed to be written by W—— S——, Esq.* First American, from the Fourth Edinburgh Edition. London: printed for James Cawthorn, 1814.
The Backwoodsman: A Poem. Philadelphia: M. Thomas, 1818.

7. Book-Length Satires (in chronological order)

The Diverting History of John Bull and Brother Jonathan, by Hector Bull-Us. New York and Philadelphia: Inskeep & Bradford; Bradford & Inskeep, 1812. 2d ed. rev. New York: Inskeep & Bradford, 1813. Revised ed. New York: Harper & Brothers, 1835. "A Critical Edition and Study of James Kirke Paulding's 'The Diverting History of John Bull and Brother Jonathan.'" Edited by Dennis D. Gartner. Ph.D. Dissertation, University of Wisconsin, 1972.
The History of a Little Frenchman and his Bank Notes: Rags! Rags! Rags! Philadelphia, [1815]. Not extant.
A Sketch of Old England by A New-England Man. 2 vols. New York: Charles Wiley, 1822. Revised ed. London: R. Phillips, 1822.
John Bull in America; or, The New Munchausen. New York: Charles Wiley, 1825.

The New Mirror for Travellers, and Guide to the Springs, by an Amateur. New York: G. and C. Carvill, 1828.

8. Treatises (in chronological order)

The United States and England: Being A Reply to the Criticism on Inchiquin's Letters, Contained in the Quarterly Review for January, 1814. New York and Philadelphia: A. H. Inskeep; Bradford & Inskeep, 1815.

Slavery in the United States. New York: Harper & Brothers, 1836.

9. Short Fiction Collections (in chronological order)

The Merry Tales of the Three Wise Men of Gotham. New York: G. and C. Carvill, 1826.

Tales of the Good Woman, by A Doubtful Gentleman. New York: G. and C. and H. Carvill, 1829. New ed. 2 vols. New York: Harper & Brothers, 1836.

Chronicles of the City of Gotham from the papers of A Retired Common Councilman. New York: G. and C. and H. Carvill, 1830.

Tales of Glauber-Spa: By Several American Authors. 2 vols. New York: J. and J. Harper, 1832. Reprint ed. New York: Garrett Press, 1969.

The Book of Saint Nicholas: Translated from the Original Dutch of Dominie Nicholas Aegidius Oudenarde. New York: Harper & Brothers, 1836 or 1837.

A Gift from Fairy Land. New York: D. Appleton & Co., 1838.

"The Uncollected Stories of James Kirke Paulding: An Annotated Edition." 3 vols. Edited by Melvin Rosser Mason. Ph.D. Dissertation, University of Texas, 1958.

10. Biography

A Life of Washington. 2 vols. New York: Harper & Brothers, 1835.

11. Collected Works.

Paulding's Works. 15 vols. New York: Harper & Brothers, 1835–1839.

12. Letters

The Letters of James Kirke Paulding. Edited by Ralph M. Aderman. Madison: University of Wisconsin Press, 1962.

SECONDARY SOURCES

1. Books

Herold, Amos L. *James Kirke Paulding: Versatile American.* New York: Columbia University Press, 1926. A brief scholarly study of Paulding's life and works, containing useful biographical and bibliographical material.

Paulding, William I. *Literary Life of James K. Paulding*. New York: Scribner & Co., 1867. A modest, apologetic memoir by the author's son, padded with quotations from the works.

2. Articles

Aderman, Ralph M. "James Kirke Paulding as Social Critic." *Papers on English Literature and Language* 1 (1965):217–29. Makes a strong case for Paulding as a thoughtful and penetrating social critic.

———. "James Kirke Paulding's Contributions to American Magazines." *Studies in Bibliography* 17 (1964):141–51. An important listing that identifies many of Paulding's anonymous contributions.

Adkins, Nelson F. "James K. Paulding's *Lion of the West*." *American Literature* 3 (November 1931):249–58. Informative study of the different versions of the play.

Conklin, W. T. "Paulding's Prose Treatment of Types and Frontier Lore Before Cooper." *University of Texas Studies in English*, no. 19 (July 8, 1939), pp. 163–71. Persuasive demonstration of Paulding's anticipation of Cooper.

Henry, Joyce. "Five More Essays by James Kirke Paulding?" *Papers of the Bibliographical Society of America* 66 (Third Quarter 1972):310–21. Presents convincing evidence that Paulding authored third version of *Lion of the West*.

Herold, Amos L. "Paulding's Literary Theories." *Bulletin of the New York Public Library* 66 (April 1962):236–43. The first recognition of Paulding's "genius" as a literary theorist.

O'Donnell, Thomas. "*Koningsmarke*: Paulding vs. Scott in 1823." *American Transcendental Quarterly*, no 24 (Fall 1974), pp. 10–17. An excellent analysis of Paulding's intentions and performance in his first novel.

Owens, Louis D. "James K. Paulding and the Foundations of American Realism." *Bulletin of the New York Public Library* 79 (Autumn 1975):40–50. An important study of Paulding's formulation of the basic tenets of Amerian literary realism.

Person, Leland S., Jr. "James Kirke Paulding: Myth and the Middle Ground." *Western American Literature* 16 (Spring 1981):39–54. A brilliant analysis of *The Dutchman's Fireside*, focusing on Paulding's creation of an "alternative myth of the wilderness."

3. Parts of Books

Cairns, William B. *British Criticism of American Writings, 1815–1833*. University of Wisconsin Studies in Language and Literature, no. 14.

Madison, 1922. Contains many useful quotations indicating the reception of Paulding's works.

Cowie, Alexander. *The Rise of the American Novel.* New York: The American Book Company, 1948. Presents a substantial, but unreliable, survey of Paulding's novels.

Duyckinck, E. A. Editor's Preface. In *Salmagundi, Irving's Works.* New York: G. P. Putnam's Sons, 1860. A sensitive, impressionistic introduction to the volume, drawing upon first-hand knowledge of the authors.

———, and Duyckinck, George L. "James Kirke Paulding." In: *The Cyclopaedia of American Literature.* Philadelphia: William Rutter & Co., 1877. A survey of Paulding's life and works. Important because Paulding helped write it.

Granger, Bruce I. "Historical Note." In: *Salmagundi.* Boston: Twayne Publishers, 1977. Contains a useful discussion of Paulding's contributions to the book.

Mansfield, Luther S. "Diversity and Innovation in the Middle States." In: *Literary History of the United States: History.* Edited by Robert E. Spiller et al. 3d ed., rev. New York: Macmillan, 1963. Contains a factually unreliable estimate of Paulding's achievement, stressing his versatility. Appears in an influential volume.

Parrington, Vernon L. *Main Currents in American Thought: Volume Two, 1800–1860, The Romantic Revolution in America.* New York: Harcourt, Brace, 1927. Presents an enthusiastic but eccentric survey, stressing Paulding's "deep-rooted agrarianism."

Taft, Kendall B. Introduction. In: *Minor Knickerbockers.* New York: American Book Co., 1947. A valuable, well-documented discussion of the Knickerbocker milieu.

Index

Abercrombie, General, 123, 124, 125, 127
Addison, 5, 24, 30
Aderman, 91, 145n17
Adventures of Huckleberry Finn, The (Twain), 76, 91
Alastor (Shelley), 73
American, The (James), 99, 102
American Monthly, 68, 73, 129
American Notebooks, The (Hawthorne), 109
American Notes (Dickens), 46
American Quarterly Review, 82, 92
American Renaissance (Matthiessen), 89
"American Scholar, The" (Emerson), 80
Analectic Magazine, 10, 60, 72, 91, 110
André, Major, 2–3, 115
"Answer to Certain Meddling Correspondents" (Irving), 25
Arbuthnot, John, 48
Arnold, General Benedict, 2
Ashe, Thomas, 41, 43
Astor, John Jacob, 74
Atlantic Souvenir, The, 13, *103–104*

Baker and Scribner, 115
Beauties of Brother Bull-Us, The, 48
Benjamin, Park, 136
Bereford, Captain John, 58
Bernard, William Bayle, 98
Bird, Henry, 71, 110–11
Blackwood's Magazine, 32, 44, 53
Boone, Daniel, 130
Bradish, Mrs., 9
Brevoort, Henry, Jr., 7, 9, 30, 33, 34, 36, 37, 39, 71–72, 129, 136
British Magazine, 118
British Review, 69
Brooks, Van Wyck, 33
Brown, Charles Brockden, 24, 75, 80
Bryant, William Cullen, 13, 30, 69, 96, 138
Byron, Lord, 32, 76, 77, 78, 88, 89, 131

Cable, 85
Calliopean Society, 7
Campbell, 44
Capote, Truman, 111
Channing, Walter, 76
Chapman, John G., 62, 136
Charles IV, 47
Charvat, William, 91–92
"Chronicles of the City of Gotham" (Irving), 29
Citizen of the World, The (Goldsmith), 4, 24
Clay, Henry, 10, 17, 117
Clemens, Samuel, 28; *See also* Twain, Mark
Cobbett, William, 41
Cockburn, Rear Admiral Sir George, *57–60*
Columbia College, 12
Columbian Magazine, 46
Conklin, W. T., 111
Cooper, James Fenimore, 40, 44, 70, 76, 79, 81, 88, 110, 113, 114, 116, 118, 124–25, 129, 137, 138
Corrector, The, 21
Cowie, Alexander, 81, 119, 126, 133

Crockett, David, 13, 85, 97

Damsel of Darien, The (Simms), 16, 137
Dana, Richard H., 29
Debating Society, The, 7
Dennie, Joseph, 24
Dickens, Charles, 46
Dickerson, Mahlon, 15
Domestic Manners of the Americans (Trollope), 45, 98, 99
Drake, Joseph Rodman, 68
Dryden, 5, 55, 86
Dunlap, William, 84
Durand, Asher, 62, 136
Duyckinck, Evert A., 32, 39, 68, 94

Eastburn, James W., 70
Edinburgh Literary Journal, 62, 69
Edinburgh Review, 44, 77
Emerson, 80, 88, 136
"English Writers on America" (Irving), 44, 77
Ensenore, 71
"Essay on Man" (Pope), 66

Fanny (Halleck), 68
Father of an Only Child (Dunlap), 84
Fessenden, Thomas Green, 23–24, 31
Fielding, 5, 90, 116, 120
Fitch, Clyde, 85
Flint, Rev. Timothy, 130
"Flummery" (William Irving), 23
Freneau, 69–70

Gifford, William, 43–44
Godey's Lady's Book, 103
Goldsmith, Oliver, 4, 5, 24, 30, 55
Goodrich, Samuel, 56, 76–77
Graham's Magazine, 72, 103
Granger, Bruce I., 25
Grant, Mrs. Anne, 124
Griswold, Rufus, 34
Gulliver's Travels (Swift), 48

Hackett, James H., 13, 85, 96, 97, 98, 137
Hall, Captain Basil, 44–45
Hall, Herold E., 50, 119
Halleck, Fitz-Greene, 68–69, 96
Harper & Brothers, 14, 16, 25
Harris, George W., 102
Hart, James D., 56, 125
Harte, 85
Havell, Robert, Jr., 62
Hawthorne (James), 79
"Hawthorne and His Mosses" (Melville), 80
Hawthorne, Nathaniel, 10, 14, 79, 88, 89, 90, 108, 109, 133, 134, 137–78
Henry, Joyce, 98
Herold, Amos L., 13, 38, 49, 54, 78, 91, 94, 104, 111, 112, 119, 125, 133
Hiawatha (Longfellow), 70
History of John Bull, The (Arbuthnot), 48
History of New York, A (Irving), 9
Hoffman, Daniel C., 147n20
Hooper, Johnson J., 102
House of the Seven Gables, The (Hawthorne), 89, 134
Howells, William Dean, 11, 19, 79, 80, 89, 91, 137
Hudson River School of Painters, 5–6, 62, 136

Inchiquin's Letters (Ingersoll), 9, 42
Ingersoll, C. Jared, 9, 42
Irving, Ebenezer, 7
Irving, Julia Paulding, 6
Irving, Pierre M., 22, 29
Irving, Peter, 7, 8

Irving, Washington, 1, 6, 7–8, 9, 10, 11, 13, 14, 15, 16, 17, 20, 21, 24, 25–26, 29, *30–35*, 36, 37, 39, 40, 41, 44, 49, 53, 60–61, 68, 71, 72, 77, 88, 91, 93, 106, 112, 116, 129, *135–36*, 137, 138
Irving, William, 6, 7, 8, 21, 24, 25, 26

Jackson, Andrew, 3, 17–18, 39, 88, 135
James I, 86
James, Henry, 11, 79, 80, 91, 99, 102, 137
Janson, Charles William, 41, 43, 50
Jarvis, John Wesley, 97
Jefferson, President, 8, 22, 25, 26, 31, 32, 52
Jeffrey, 44
Jewett, 85
"John Bull" (Irving), 49
Johnson, Sir William, 122, 123, 124, 125, 127, 128

Kean, Charles, 83
Kean, Edmund, 83
Keiser, Albert, 119
Kelly, Lydia, 83
Kemble, Charles, 83
Kemble, Fanny, 83
Kemble, Gertrude, 11; *See also* Paulding, Gertrude
Kemble, Peter, 11
King, Philip, 72
Knickerbocker Magazine, 91

Lads of Kilkenny, 7
Lady of the Lake, The (Scott), 56
Lady's Magazine, 53
Lambert, John, 30
Lay of the Last Minstrel, The (Scott), 9, 42, 55, 56, 59
Leaves of Grass (Whitman), 76, 80–81
"Legend of Sleepy Hollow, The" (Irving), 34, 106
Life on the Mississippi (Twain), 56
Literary Examiner, 118
Literary Gazette, 53, 118
Literary History of the United States, 69
Literary Life (W. I. Paulding), 31
Literary Magazine, 24
Literary World, The, 32
"Little Man in Black, The" (Irving), 29
Longfellow, 71
Longworth, David, *21*, 26, 29, 31
Louis XVI, 47
Lovelace, Governor, 118

Macbeth (Shakespeare), 22
McCall, Richard, 7
M'Donald, Randall, 111
Macready, William Charles, 83
Madison, President, 10, 39, 48, 61, 135
Mailer, Norman, 111
Mansfield, Luther S., 49
Marble Faun, The (Hawthorne), 79
Mardi (Melville), 49
Marmion (Scott), 56
Mason, Melvin R., 99, 103
Matthiessen, F. O., 89
Mead, Charles, 70
Melville, Herman, 10, 19, 49, 63, 80, 88, 136
Memoirs of an American Lady (Grant), 124
Miller, Arthur, 85
Milton, 86
Minerva, 118
Miscellaneous Works (Freneau), 69–70
Mississippian Scenery (Mead), 70
Moby-Dick (Melville), 35, 67, 76, 89

Monroe, President, 12
Monthly Magazine, 53
Monthly Review, 69
Moore, Thomas, 22, 44, 77, 89
Morning Chronicle, 8, 21
Morris, George P., 19
Morton, Sarah Wentworth, 70

Napier, Sir Charles, 57
Napoleon, 47
Narrative of Arthur Gordon Pym, The (Poe), 137
Nation, 138
Neal, John, 32, 53, 125
Nevins, Allan, 41
New England Magazine, 125, 129
New York Courier & Enquirer, 16
New York Evening Post, 15, 17, 68
New-York Mirror, 13, 45, 72, 96, 97, 98, 103, 118, 125, 129
News of Literature and Fashion, 53
North American Review, 75–76, 79
Notions of the Americans (Cooper), 79

O'Donnell, Thomas F., 82, 119, 125
Ogden, Henry, 7
Ogden, Nathaniel (JKP's grandfather), 2
Oldstyle, Jonathan, 8, 21
"On Greatness" (Irving), 25, 31
O'Neill, Eugene, 85
O'Neill, John, 57, 59–60
Orians, G. Harrison, 81
Origins of American Critical Thought, The (Charvat), 91–92
Othello (Shakespeare), 36
Ouâbi (Morton), 70
Owen, Robert, 13
Owens, Louis D., 85

Paine, Thomas, 32
Paper War, The, 9, 32, *40–46*, 49, 53, 54, 75

Parrington, Vernon L., 119, 125
Pattee, Fred Lewis, 33, 103
Paulding, Catharine Ogden (JKP's mother), 4, 5, 12
Paulding, Gertrude (JKP's wife), 74, 116; *See also* Kemble, Gertrude
Paulding, James Kirke, abuse at hands of critics, 16, 32–33, 35, 61, 68, 136, 138; admiration for Jackson, 17–18; admiration for John Paulding, 2–3, 114; and Irving, *6–8*, 9–10, 20, 25–26, *30–35*, 39–40, 44, 60–61, 77, 93, 112, *136*; and Scott, 55–56, 60, 87; and the Hudson River Valley, 1, 5–6, 18, 62, 136; and the Indian, 12, *62–63*, *70–72*, 110–11, 117–18, 134, 136; and the Revolution, 1–3, 114; and the War of 1812, 56–57; anglophobia, 1, 12, 39, 56, 78; bias against New England, 18, 60, 102, 115; bias toward the South, 11, 14–15, 102; careless writing, 55, 73, 103, 113, 115–16; character, 12–13, 14–15, 16, 135; childhood and youth, 1–6; criticism of religious fanaticism, 5, 132–33; education, 4, 7; eighteenth-century influences, 4–5, 24, 48–49, 55, 94, 116, 120, 128; in New York City, 6–8; literary realism, 1, 79–80, 90–91; love of nature, 5–6, 28, 136; marriage, 11; nationalism, 1, *39–40*, 75–78, 80–81, 93–94; participation in the Paper War, 9–12, *40–46*; poverty, 3–4, 135; psychological realism, 14, 109, 129, 135; reign as popular author, 12–15, 111, 129; reputation, 19, 20, 34, 129, 135–38; retirement, 17–19; service as Secretary of the Navy, 16–17; ties

to the New York Dutch, *1*, 103, 105, 121–28, 137

WORKS: PLAYS:
American Comedies, 18
Bucktails, The, 18, 42, 93, *94–96*
Fanaticism and Hypocrisy, 94
Kentuckian, The, 98; *See also The Lion of the West*
Lion of the West, The, 13, 46, 82, 85, 93, 94, *96–102*, 113, 137, 138
Sea Nymph, 94

WORKS: POETRY:
Backwoodsman, The, 3, 11, 55, *61–74*, 76, 81, 93, 129, 136, 138
"Battle of Erie," 73
"Dreaming Oddity, A," 73
Lay of the Scottish Fiddle, The, 9, 42, *55–61*, 72
"Ode on the National Apathy," 73
"Sailor's Elegy on the Fate of the Wasp, A," 73
"Stripes and Stars," 73
"Volunteer, The," 73
"White Man and the Red Man, The," 73

WORKS: PROSE
"Adventures of Henry Bird, The," 71, 103, *110–11*
"Advertisement," 25
"American Drama," 78, *82–85*, 86, 91, 93
"Art of Living, The," 37
"Autumnal Reflections," 25, 26, *28–29*, 32
Book of St. Nicholas, The, 15
"Character of Pindar Cockloft," 25
"Childe Roeliffe's Pilgrimage," 103, *109–10*
Chronicles of the City of Gotham, 13
"Cobus Yerks," 1, 103, 104, *106–108*, 138
"Codification," 36
"Country Village, The," 37
"Criticism," 36
Diverting History of John Bull and Brother Jonathan, The, 9, 42, 45, *46–49*
Dutchman's Fireside, The, 1, 13–14, 81, 113, *121–28*, 129, 132, 134, 138
"Dumb Girl, The," 5, 103, *108–109*, 138
"Dyspepsy," 3, 5
Gift from Fairy Land, A, 15
History of the Little Frenchman, The, 10
"*—How now mooncalf*!," 25
"Illinois and the Prairies, The," 18
John Bull in America, 13, 44, 46, *49–54*, 135, 138
Koningsmarke, 12, 71, 113, *116–20*, 121
"Leaves from Mrs. Trollope's Journal," 45, 98
"Letter from Demy Semiquaver," 25
Letters from the South, 11, 43–44, 85
Life of Washington, A, 14
"Little Dutch Sentinel of the Manhadoes, The," 1, 103, *104–106*
"Memorandums for a Tour," 41
Merry Tales of the Three Wise Men, The, 13
"Mine Uncle John," 25, *26–27*, 32
"Mr. Wilson's Concert," 25

"Mississippi, The," 18
"Mother's Tragedy, The," 5, 111
"National Literature," 11, 37, *78–82*, 84, 85, 86, 90, 92
New Mirror for Travellers, The, 3, 13
"Notes, by William Wizard," 25
Old Continental, The, 3, 18, 113, *114–15*, 132
"Old Ferry House, The," 37
"On the Influence of Foreign Literature," 37, 44
"Peter Pettifog, the Great Traveller," 46
"Poor Genevieve," 111
Puritan and His Daughter, The, 18, 113, *115–16*
"Retrospect, A," 25, 26, *27–28*
Salmagundi, 8, 11, *20–35*, 41, 42, 135–36, 138
Salmagundi, Second Series, 8, 11, *35–38*, 44, 78, 141n35
"Signs of the Times," 37
Sketch of Old England, A, 11, 44, 53, 78, 87
"Sketch of the Great Western Lakes," 18
"Sketches from Nature," 25
Slavery in the United States, 14–15
"Stranger at Home, The," 25
"Stranger in New Jersey, The," 25
"Style at Ballston," 25
Tales of Glauber-Spa, 13, 109
Tales of the Good Woman, 13
"Theatrics," 22
"Town and Country," 37
"Uncollected Stories, The," 103
United States and England, The, 9, 10, 43, 75
Westward Ho!, 2, 5, 14, 45, 113, *129–34*
"White Indian, The," 111
"Wise Conjectures of the Town," 25
"Wreck of Genius, The," 11, 37, 78
"York Town," 77, 78, 82, *85–91*

Paulding, John (JKP's cousin), *2–3*, 18, 114
Paulding, Joost or Joseph (JKP's grandfather), 1
Paulding, Mary Kemble (1824–1827) (JKP's daughter), 12
Paulding, Mary Kemble (1827–1828), (JKP's daughter), 12
Paulding, Sarah (JKP's aunt), 2
Paulding, William, Jr. (JKP's brother), 6, 12
Paulding, William, Sr. (JKP's father), 1, 3–4, 12
Paulding, William Irving (1821–1825) (JKP's son), 12, 53
Paulding, William Irving (1825–1890) (JKP's son), 18, 19, 138
Pearce, Roy Harvey, 70, 98
Pedlar, The (Wetmore), 102
Penn, William, 118
Percival, 69
Person, Leland S., Jr., 126
"Philip of Pokanoket" (Irving), 72
Pioneers, The (Cooper), 70, 81
Pirate, The (Scott), 116
Pitt, William, 47
Poe, Edgar Allan, 14, 135, 137
Poinsett, Joel, 17
Polk, 18
Pope, 5, 55, 66, 86
Port Folio, 24
Porter, David, 7
Precaution (Cooper), 76

Quarterly Review, 9, 42, 43, 44, 51, 53, 61
Quincy, John, 60
Quinn, Arthur Hobson, 83, 84, 125

Rabelais, 24
Randolph, John, 10
Recollections (Flint), 130
Requa, Isaac, 2
Robertson, James Holman, 119, 125

"SALMAGUNDI—*alias* BUBBLE AND SQUEAK" (Fessenden), 23
Sands, Robert C., 70
Sanillac (Whiting), 70
Satanstoe (Cooper), 124
Scarlet Letter, The (Hawthorne), 76, 91, 108, 109, 138
Scott, Sir Walter, 9, 12, 42, 44, *55–60*, 76, 77, 78, 87, 92, 116
Sedgwick, Catharine M., 13
Shakespeare, 83, 86–87
Shelley, 73
Sheridan, 83
Simms, William Gilmore, 16, 113, 137
Simon Sugg's Adventures (Hooper), 102
Sketch Book, The (Irving), 9, 11, 33, 35, 44, 72, 77
Sketches and Eccentricities of Col. David Crockett, 101
Smith, Sydney, 44, 77
Southern Literary Messenger, 77, 78
Specimens of the American Poets, 69
Spectator, The, 24
Speculation, 93
Spenser, 86
Spy, The (Cooper), 18, 81, 114
Stone, John Augustus, 97–98
Storer, George L., 12
Stranger in America, The (Janson), 50
Sut Lovingood's Yarns (Harris), 102
Swift, 5, 24, 48–49

Tales of a Traveller (Irving), 34
Tallmadge, Colonel Benjamin, 2–3
Tecumseh, 63, 64, 71
Tenskwatawa (the Prophet), 63, 71
Thomas, Augustus, 85
Thomas, Moses, 35
Thoreau, 88
Tidwell, James N., 98
Tom Jones (Fielding), 12, 16
Town, 21
"Traits of Indian Character" (Irving), 72
Travels in North America (Hall), 44
Trollope, Francis M., 45–46, 48, 98
Turner, Arlin, 130
Twain, Mark, 10, 11, 56, 79, 80, 85, 91, 131, 137; *See also* Clemens, Samuel
Tyler, Royall, 75

Van Buren, Martin, 15, 16, 17, 18, 39, 135
Van Wart, Isaac, 2

Warren, Admiral Sir John, 57
Washington, George, 8, 14
Washington, Globe, 17
Watkins, Floyd C., 54, 95, 125
Webb, Colonel James Watson, 16
Weekly Inspector, 23
Weir, John Ferguson, 62
Weir, Robert W., 62, 136
Weld, Isaac, 41
Westminster Review, 125
Wetmore, Alphonso, 102
White, E. B., 27
Whiting, Henry, 70
Whitman, 10, 80, 88, 136–37
Wilkes, Charles, 16–17
Williams, David, 2
Williams, Stanley T., 26

Williams, Tennessee, 85
Willis, N. P., 16, 33, 74, 136
Wilson, James Grant, 74
Withers, Walter, 8
Wordsworth, 78, 87

Yamoyden (Eastburn and Sands), 70
"Young Goodman Brown" (Hawthorne), 91